JUSTICE

ON THE

Ropes

RUBIN "HURRICANE" CARTER, FRED W. HOGAN, JOHN ARTIS AND THE WRONGFUL CONVICTION MOVEMENT

BY JEFF BEACH AND FRED W. HOGAN

Dedications

Jeff – For Nicolette Shannon and Holly Leigh, the only two things I've ever helped create that bring me more pride than this book. Love you both.

Fred – For Lauren, truly the love of my life, who loves, and is loved by me, with absolute support and devotion for each other, and without whom this book couldn't have been written. And for David and Matthew. Their mother and I are extremely proud of the men they have grown to be, and who have blessed us with seven grandchildren between them.

Table of Contents

Foreword

What can I say about Fred Hogan, his work to prove Rubin Carter and me innocent in the Lafayette Bar and Grille murder case, and the work that Fred, Rubin and I have done since then to help those who were wrongfully convicted?

That is a tough one. How do you say, in just a few paragraphs, what it means to have someone believe in you so thoroughly that they will spend hours upon hours working to prove you were wrongfully convicted? Someone from a completely different background from yours. Someone who just as easily could have been on the other side of the courtroom, if he had continued in his job as a police officer and not become an investigator for the Public Defender's Office. Someone who had no reason to fight for you other than this: He saw an injustice and was determined to correct it.

If it had been just "his job," and he was only doing what his bosses told him to do, well, that would be one thing. But Rubin and I weren't Public Defender's Office clients. Nobody was paying Fred to dig into our case the way he did, all in his spare time. He did it out of a sense of setting things right.

And it didn't begin and end with his work on the case. He was there to serve as my chaperon when I became the first lifer to be allowed out on a "furlough" in New Jersey. He was there to serve as my best man when I got married while still in prison. He's been there for the many times I've been invited to gatherings of people looking to exonerate the wrongfully convicted.

I suppose that's why our relationship carried on beyond the end of the Lafayette Bar and Grille case. After I had been freed from prison. After Judge Sarokin overturned my and Rubin's convictions, and Rubin joined me as a free man. Fred also was there, shoulder-to-shoulder, when Rubin was afflicted with cancer toward the end of his days and when he wanted nothing more than to spend what time he had left with people who had been important in his life.

I thought a lot about those times when Fred and I took a trip in 2016 down the Mississippi Delta. Rubin, whose boxing career and his work as a crusader for the wrongfully convicted took him all over the world, had always wanted to travel in the footsteps of the great Mississippi bluesmen whose music so perfectly captured what it meant to be downtrodden and to face incredible odds just to survive. He never got to make that trip, and once the cancer took hold of him, he was no longer able.

We spread some of Rubin's ashes in notable places along that route when Fred and I took the trip Rubin never got to take, including at the famous "Crossroads," where legend holds that Robert Johnson sold his soul to the Devil for musical success. We spread some at "Ground Zero," a jazz club co-owned by Morgan Freeman, where I got the chance to play drums. And I felt a special connection to Rubin's love for Delta blues at Po' Monkey's, the last true "juke joint" in the Deep South, situated in an old sharecropper's house.

Fred and I are both in our 70s now. Time, as it does, has taken its toll. We've both faced down more than our fair share of demons, both internal ones and those that come at us from the outside. Through everything, the one thing I never questioned was my friendship with Fred Hogan.

I hope this book will be a time capsule, so to speak, of the years since Fred, Rubin and I first met behind bars to talk about reversing the injustice that was the Lafayette Bar and Grille triple murder case. More so, I hope it shows the work we three collaborated on to dig deep into the inequities of the justice system.

And most of all, I hope it serves as a lesson about how three very different men, bonded by lifelong friendship and a commitment to justice, can make a difference in the world.

--- John Artis

ONE

A Prison Riot Strengthens Friendship for Investigator and Inmates

(Thanksgiving 1971: Five-and-a-half years after the Lafayette Bar and Grille triple murder)

Fred Hogan had been working with Rubin "Hurricane" Carter and John Artis for months, with an eye toward exonerating them in a 1966 triple murder, when a riot broke out in the prison where both men were housed. Their interaction during and immediately after the riot strengthened the bond that had been growing as Hogan sought information that could overturn their convictions.

Fred Hogan cautiously slid out of the car and surveyed the chaotic riot scene before him. He could see pockets of fire coming from the institution the locals called "Rahway State Prison," smoke billowing into the cool November night. Signs written by inmates on bedsheets were hanging from between the barred windows. Police by the dozens, if not hundreds (it was hard to tell in all the confusion) gathered outside, awaiting orders to take back the prison by force.

All the cliches from a James Cagney or Burt Lancaster film, come to life and close enough to touch.

Hogan, a first-year investigator for the New Jersey Office of the Public Defender, couldn't help but notice the contrast to the relaxing Thanksgiving he'd been spending just a few hours before. Before the call from Bill Gearty, the Deputy Public Defender for Monmouth County, New Jersey, who was Hogan's county-level boss.

To be sure, this wasn't Hogan's first rodeo in the midst of a riot. Just a few years earlier, as a young officer in the Atlantic Highlands Police Department, he'd been sent to help quell the riots in Asbury Park, a town that, at the time, was known as a declining beach resort, before Springsteen made it famous again for a whole new set of reasons.

"Fred and I were shoulder-to shoulder during those riots," said Ken Grover, a former police sergeant and a retired director of security for Public Service Electric and Gas (PSE&G), one of New Jersey's largest utilities. Grover was Hogan's partner during his brief stint in the Atlantic Highlands Police Department before Hogan's move to the Public Defender's Office. "They (rioters) beat us down for two, three days. It was a rude awakening for me. In college, I had seen pictures of the riots in Newark and saw (police officers) with their nightsticks raised, and I promised myself I wasn't going to become one of **those** cops. When we were in the middle of those (Asbury Park) riots, I realized pretty quickly that I was lying to myself."

Fred Hogan and Ken Grover

This was indeed a time in New Jersey's history, and the history of the nation, when the peace-and-love ethos of the '60s was giving way to the anger and turmoil of the early-'70s. Riots in urban areas were among the most common, and certainly the most headline-grabbing, manifestations of that change.

And when the Thanksgiving 1971 riot broke out at the prison in Rahway, now officially known as East Jersey State Prison, the state's leaders were all too cognizant of a similar uprising in New York State just a few months before, which had left the bodies of 39 people – 10 guards and civilians, along with 29 inmates – strewn throughout a prison. All they could think in New Jersey was, "We don't need another Attica here."

Adding to the potential for public scrutiny of the Rahway riot was the high profile of two of the inmates housed there at that time, Rubin

"Hurricane" Carter and John Artis. The two men had been convicted in a triple murder at the Lafayette Bar and Grille in Paterson, New Jersey, and the case had drawn the attention of the media because of the racial component (the victims were all white, and "eyewitnesses" had said both shooters were black) and because Carter was well known as a professional middleweight boxer when he was charged.

Carter also had become known as an outspoken critic of the police and their contentious relationship with the African-American community – some claim he encouraged inner-city residents to physically attack police – which others maintain to this day was the reason he was fingered as a suspect in the barroom massacre in the first place. Hogan was keenly aware of Carter's presence at Rahway, as he had been visiting the inmate to talk about what Hogan felt was a miscarriage of justice in the Lafayette case. A fan of Carter's as a youth, Hogan had once had the opportunity to spar with the boxer at his training camp when Hogan was a 16-year-old Police Athletic League pugilist. Although Carter was not a Public Defender client, Hogan had used his own time to visit him and discuss the potential for raising questions about the boxer's innocence, as well as that of his co-defendant, John Artis, at the time a high school track-and-field standout. Hogan was, as Carter wrote to Hogan in signing a copy of Carter's first book, "the beginning."

In the immediate moment, however, Hogan's concerns were not so much about Carter's case, but about the safety of his friend and all the inmates and prison staff, as the scene at Rahway looked to be spiraling out of control.

"We pulled up and we saw the signs hanging out of the prison," Hogan recalls. "It looked like things were burning. It looked like tear gas had been fired. The State Police were there. It wasn't quite clear when or if they were gonna storm the place. Hostages had been taken, including the warden. It all started as a drunken stupor on jailhouse hooch and it just got out of hand from there. Inmates started saying, let's do this and let's do that. They were grabbing people to hold hostage. And before you know it, they were like, 'Holy shit! What did we do?'"

East Jersey State Prison ("Rahway Prison")

In the aftermath of the riot, both Carter and Artis would be credited by various sources as having helped some of the prison guards escape what might have been deadly "street justice" meted out by inmates. Artis recalls that, "I had heard these guys (inmates) talking about how they were gonna kill some guards. So I got to the guards and told them, 'C'mon, we've gotta get you out of here.' It was one of the main reasons I was paroled when I was." (Artis actually was paroled **before** his and Carter's convictions were overturned by a federal judge, a striking fact considering he was serving three concurrent life sentences.)

Hogan, who had begun before the riot visiting both men to talk about seeking ways to exonerate them, was obviously aware of their presence amid the dangerous scene, but also felt they could command the respect of fellow inmates enough to help avoid a repeat of Attica.

"The first thing that happened was (the authorities) shut off the electricity and the water," Hogan recalls. "Some of the inmates started being juvenile and were wrecking the place out of frustration. Rubin told people, 'Go back to your cells, get as much water out of your toilets as you can and secure yourselves, because before you know it, some shit's gonna start happening.'"

It was partly because of Carter, and his co-defendant Artis, that Hogan had cut his Thanksgiving evening short. Hogan and Carter, and by extension Artis, had become fast friends since Hogan had left the Atlantic Highlands Police Department to go to work for the state's Office of the Public Defender.

In responding to the riot, the team put together by then-Public Defender Stanley Van Ness soon learned what their investigative member had already realized. The man convicted of the brutal murders at the Lafayette (later to be convicted a second time before finally being exonerated) did not match up with the person they came to know.

"The first day we went back to Rahway after the riot," Bill Gearty recalls, "I'm up there sitting at a table and we're talking to Carter, and a guard comes over, very unobtrusively, and walks around and places his hand on Carter's shoulder. And he just says, 'Thanks,' and leaves, and Carter just kind of nods. Apparently, one of the prisoners (during the riot) was about to do this guard in and Carter picked the guy up and threw him a quarter-mile, or whatever he did, to save this guard."

While it may have taken the attorneys by surprise, the act of kindness was completely in character for the Carter with whom Hogan had built a friendship and who later would become the stuff of legend in song, Bob Dylan's "The Hurricane," and film, 1999's "Hurricane," starring Denzel Washington, and an author of multiple books detailing the charges against him, his fight for vindication, and the larger issues of equality and justice that his and Artis' cases personified.

What the inmates had done on that cold Thanksgiving evening quickly drew the attention of then-Governor William T. Cahill, who wanted desperately to avoid a repeat of the bloodshed and national outrage that resulted from Attica. To that end, Governor Cahill had assured the inmates he would take seriously their long list of complaints about the prison – everything from the quality of the food (calling that quality "low" would have been generous) to a lack of vocational and educational programs, to random retribution from guards – and had called on Public Defender Stanley Van Ness to put together a team to go to Rahway and work as liaisons to the inmates.

When Van Ness called Gearty at home that Thanksgiving to ask him to take himself, another NJOPD attorney and an investigator to the riot, Van Ness didn't need to say much more, and didn't. As only the second statewide Public Defender in New Jersey history (the first had committed suicide by leaping from a bridge) and the state's first-ever African-American member of a governor's cabinet, Van Ness had quickly earned the respect of the lawyers, investigators and other staff in the fledgling legal-defense operation.

So Gearty reached out to attorney David Foley from the Monmouth office to fill the attorney's spot. When it came to the investigator, he knew immediately whom he wanted to call.

"I got along well with Freddy (Hogan) and respected him and his innovative way of doing things and the initiative he showed," Gearty says. "He was the kind of person you didn't have to tell what to do each step of the way. He just did it. You'd read his reports and everything was already there."

And so, the three left behind their holidays and made their way to the scene of what would later become known as New Jersey's most famous prison riot, not the least reason for which was the presence of one inmate who would soon become known worldwide. While they spent most of that night "not doing a whole lot of anything," according to their recollection, they would, in the days following the riot, set up shop in the prison, recording the grievances of inmates and generally trying to make good on Cahill's promise to take the issue of prison reform seriously. The two men who would record those grievances in an oversized, hard-bound, hand-written ledger would be Hogan and Carter. Hogan has kept that ledger to this day.

"As I was leaving the prison with Foley and Hogan after the riot, we met the Governor coming out," Gearty says. "Governor Cahill walked out of the building with no one getting hurt and no one dying and the physical damage to the property being the worst thing. I think they learned from the mistakes of Attica."

The inmates, too, may have had the news of that recent prison debacle on their minds. Looking at the sea of cops swelling outside the prison, the inmates began to realize that theirs was a losing cause, even if they didn't quite want to admit it yet. They had a few cards left to play, having taken the warden and several others hostage. They were pretty sure police wouldn't want to endanger those people, so they decided to at least take a stand to improve conditions at Rahway.

Like most maximum security prisons of the time, Rahway, which actually sits in the Avenel section of neighboring Woodbridge Township (the confusion over the town name is a definite sore spot for Rahway residents), was little more than a place to warehouse the most hardcore of New Jersey's criminals. Little thought was given to how they might be prepared to re-enter society once their long years of being brutalized by bigger, stronger and tougher inmates, as well as by some guards, would come to an end. The fact that Rahway didn't end the way Attica did is regarded as something of a minor miracle.

The Rahway riot, and the efforts toward prison reform in New Jersey, would serve as yet another in a series of events that brought Hogan, Carter and Artis' lives to an intersection over more than 50 years before Carter's death in April 2014. A series of seemingly unrelated events that fell into each other like dominoes over the decades, often with the result being a step forward in a criminal justice reform movement in New Jersey and elsewhere that may have looked entirely different had the men never met, never become friends.

Hogan first learned of the charges brought against his boxing idol while serving in the Army in Germany. He had received training at Fort Polk, Louisiana, aka. "Tigerland," a tropically hot outpost that served as a grist mill for young men to get them used to the conditions they would face in Vietnam, a country and conflict most were unfamiliar with, and from which many would never return.

Hogan's father had sent him newspaper clippings from the *Newark Star-Ledger* and the *Jersey Journal* about Carter and Artis being charged with the triple homicides at the Lafayette. More clippings followed, right up through the conviction of the two men on all counts.

"When the convictions happened, I didn't believe it," Hogan recalls. "I thought, 'Holy shit! This doesn't sound right.' Incrementally, there'd be something in the papers about their appeals. It just didn't sit right. According to the eyewitnesses, it was the taller of the two, which would've been John, if you believed it was these two guys, who had done more of the damage. But when they were sentenced, Rubin got three life terms, two consecutive, and John got three life terms, all of them running concurrent. Why would the person who supposedly did more of the damage get the lesser sentence? It just didn't sit right."

And so the seeds were sown as Hogan served his tour of duty with a NATO unit. He had been lucky with that assignment. Tigerland sent more young men into Vietnam than any training base in the United States. Far from the sweltering heat and humidity of Beauregard Parish, Louisiana, Hogan had time to read and think about the highly suspect conviction of a man who had taken time from the busy schedule of a professional boxer to tutor him on the finer points of the "sweet science."

The former boxer, wrongfully accused and convicted and incarcerated, and then ultimately exonerated and lionized. His "accomplice," at the time of the crime a 19-year-old star high-school athlete with a clean criminal record and dreams of Olympic track-and-field glory. The quintessential man who is at the wrong place at the wrong time. And the stocky, fast-talking, Serpico-mustachioed, 26-year-old "kid" from the Public Defender's Office.

Though they couldn't have known it when they first met, their lives together would have a major impact on criminal justice and prison reform, not only in New Jersey, but throughout the United States, into Canada and beyond. If "Jersey Justice" created an environment in which two men could be accused and then twice convicted of a horrific triple murder all because of what the federal judge who later reversed their convictions called "prosecutorial misconduct and racial revenge," then it is only fitting that the fight to rectify that one instance of injustice would later blossom into a nationwide and even international movement to spare others the same fate.

Is it a story of incredible coincidence? Or was there some larger force at work that kept bringing them back together throughout their lives?

Fred Hogan and Rubin "Hurricane" Carter

TWO

Boxing Encounter Brings Two Very Different People Together

(Circa Early-1964: About two-and-a-half years before the Lafayette Bar and Grille triple murder)

Fred Hogan and Rubin Carter had met even before the fateful triple murder at the Lafayette Bar and Grille in Paterson, New Jersey. Had their first encounter never happened, the rest of this story might have unfolded in a completely different way, or perhaps not unfolded at all. The following chapter examines the very different backgrounds of the two men, and that one chance meeting that set the rest of their 50-plus-year friendship in motion.

The story of how Fred Hogan, Rubin Carter and John Artis would combine to become agents of change in the criminal justice system did not begin with the three men meeting in a New Jersey state prison to discuss a triple-murder case. It did not even begin on the night of that triple murder itself.

It began in a boxing ring.

Fred Hogan's first encounter with Rubin Carter, the man who later became world-famous for his fight for freedom more so than for his fights in the ring, was about two years before Carter and co-defendant John Artis were charged with gunning down three people at the Lafayette Bar and Grille in Paterson, New Jersey.

In the early-1960s, Hogan's father was a correctional officer at the Hudson County Jail in Jersey City. Employed as the jail's deputy warden at the time was a man named Pat Amato. On the side, Amato doubled as a boxing manager, and one of his charges was Rubin "Hurricane" Carter.

"Pat Amato also ran the Police Athletic League in (nearby) Bayonne," Hogan recalls. "And he'd have all us kids go through our paces and get in the ring and he'd show us what boxing was all about. So one day, I got the opportunity to go up to Rubin's training camp up in Chatham, New Jersey. Well, when I first met Rubin, and this was in the latter part of '63 or early in '64, oh man, was he an impressive guy! The bald head, the goatee. That was uncharacteristic of anybody else at the time. No sports figure of that time looked like that. He was really the first one to cultivate that look. That was his signature appearance.

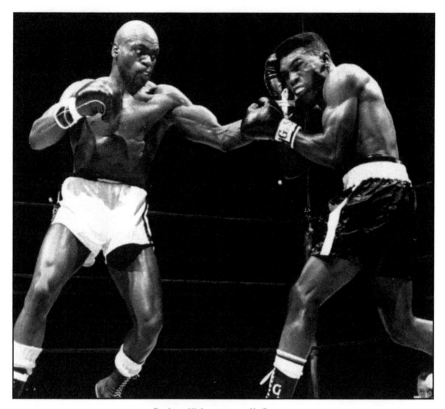

Rubin "Hurricane" Carter

"So I got in the ring with him, did a little sparring, he showed me some moves. He was very engaging. I had a good day with him. We met some other fighters, did some roadwork. He gave me a poster for a fight he had upcoming. And, after that, I always followed his career as a fan."

When you see videos of Carter's fights, you understand immediately how he got the nickname "Hurricane." The middleweight carried himself more like a heavyweight, with lightning-fast fists packed with thunderous punching power. He rarely weighed more than 160 pounds, but it was solid muscle, making him look bigger than his weight class. It was not unheard of to see him knock an opponent clear through the ropes with just a couple blows. About the easiest way to get today's audience to imagine what a Rubin Carter fight looked like is to say that he was the Mike Tyson of his day. Only, as a middleweight, quite a bit faster. His career would end, with his arrest in the Lafayette Bar and Grille case, with a professional record of 27-12-1, not overwhelming by today's standards, but respectable. The true ferocity of his ring style can't be discerned by looking at the record books. It has to be seen on tape to be believed.

As for a future for himself in the fight game, Hogan says, boxing "was something that I realized I didn't want to do with any great regularity."

And so, it seemed at the time, the contact between the two was brief, if memorable, for the teenager, but certainly not anything that foretold a lifelong friendship.

That probably could have been expected, given the vast differences in their backgrounds. While Hogan was the son of a county jail officer, Carter had spent much of his youth on the other side of the bars. By the time Carter was becoming known as a premier middleweight boxer, he was gaining nearly as much notoriety for speaking out about the violence enveloping urban areas. He went so far as to advocate people taking up arms against the police, and many would later ascribe the murder prosecutions against him and John Artis as being motivated, at least in part, by those statements.

According to numerous books, including his prison-penned autobiography "The Sixteenth Round," Carter was in trouble with the law by the time he was 11. Before long, he found himself incarcerated at the Jamesburg Youth Correctional Facility, alternately known as the New Jersey Training School for Boys, an old-style reform school intended to set wayward kids on a better path by whatever means necessary. Carter would spend most of his youth there, and while he frequently found himself at odds with guards and other officials, he did find fulfillment in one aspect of life in Jamesburg — working on the facility's farm.

In *"Eye of the Hurricane: My Path from Darkness to Freedom,"* Carter wrote about the peace he found on the farm, especially when working with the facility's dairy herd, and he saw the opportunity in that setting to learn:

That barn was a one-room schoolhouse. One of my cows, Number 319, was a real kicker. She slammed more than one person into the barn wall. I had to put her in leg braces and shackles to tie her down. Mr. Hart made sure that I had all the bad cows, not as a punishment, but because I was so good at handling them. That was my psychology class. ("Eye of the Hurricane: My Path from Darkness to Freedom" by Dr. Rubin "Hurricane" Carter with Ken Klosky. Lawrence Hill Books. 2011.)

Eventually, Carter would run away from Jamesburg, along with two other young men, in 1954. While the other two were captured, Carter eluded authorities, made his way first to Newark, then to New York City and then Philadelphia before enlisting in the Army, hiding his true identity from recruiters by saying he was from Philadelphia, where he had been staying with a cousin.

By contrast, Hogan's upbringing was one in which family and neighborhood, not government institutions, provided the guiding structure. Though Jersey City as a whole in that time was generally integrated, the neighborhoods were still clearly segregated, with Italians, Irish, Eastern Europeans and African-Americans each having their respective boundaries.

"In those days, the neighborhood cops would walk the beat," Hogan recalls, "and if you were standing on the corner, a cop might come along and say, 'This is my corner, get off the corner,' and if you didn't, you'd get a kick in the ass or hit with a nightstick. Anytime you were out of your neighborhood, the cop would say, 'This isn't your neighborhood. You don't belong here.' We didn't see it as a racist thing. It was just a neighborhood thing."

He describes a young life that sounds like something out of a Bowery Boys movie.

"Down the street, there were the four Shanley Brothers. One was a priest, another owned the saloon, and two were iron workers who also boxed professionally. Every Friday night, Mr. Shanley would get a load on, come home and get the shit kicked out of him, his wife would hit him with something, and an ambulance would be called. But come Sunday morning, (they'd be) arm-in-arm, on their way to church, 'Top of the morning to ya.'"

Fred Hogan (right) and his parents, Varna and Dotty.

In the home of Dorothy and Varna "Sonny" Hogan, there was an expectation of strict adherence to the rules of the house.

"One night my father came home after a 4-to-12 shift. He woke me up and said, 'Downstairs, now!' I thought the place was on fire. I said, 'What's up, Pop?' He says, 'That your cereal bowl in the sink? Who do you think is gonna clean it up?' I just said, 'Me, Pop.' You didn't question. When I got married, my wife was from a family of seven kids. Her parents were happy if the bowl *made* it to the sink."

Besides working as a jail guard, the elder Hogan, known alternately as "Sonny" or "Barney," also held a second job "down on the docks." His wife stayed at home until their children, Fred and his older sister, Carol, were about 8 and 10, respectively, and then Dorothy went to work for RCA in Jersey City.

"Me and my sister were what today would be referred to as 'latchkey kids,'" he says. "That term didn't exist back then. You just came home from school, waited until your parents got home, and don't get caught doing anything stupid, and that was that."

By his early-teens, after bouts with asthma and allergies (one effective remedy for which was being held upside down from the second-story window of his brownstone home to help him catch his breath), Hogan was shining shoes, making deliveries, hawking newspapers such as the *Hudson Dispatch*, "for a guy named 'Newsboy Moriarty,' who had newsstands all over the place," basically doing any job that could turn a buck or two. Along the way, he developed the fast-talking chatter that would become one of his signatures, one of the reasons Carter referred to him affectionately as "The Chipmunk."

Frank DeSevo, a New Jersey defense attorney who later would represent Hogan in one of the many actions related to the Carter case, grew up about three years ahead of Hogan in the same neighborhood, and recalls it as a place where street smarts were more valuable than formal education and where legal training included the value of an eyewitness.

"I had basically been thrown out of Don Bosco (Preparatory School); had to get out of there, it was like a prison," DeSevo remembers. "And I started hanging around in the neighborhood with some guys who were not the finest of characters. There were five bars within a block of your house, so you'd go out and make the rounds. There were always fights in the clubs.

"One guy, I remember, he was going out with this girl and he goes over to her house and there's a sign on the door that says, 'Door broken. Go around back.' So he goes around back and he gets shot three times. She ID'd the people who did it on Thursday. By Monday, somebody had gotten to her and she's like, 'Well, I don't know, I'm not sure.' They all get acquitted."

In that environment, Hogan learned the value of talking fast and always having a story to tell. Though they'd yet to meet, it was a sharp contrast to Carter, whose battle with a stutter often led him to say little, if anything, for fear of sounding out-of-place.

In later life, perhaps influenced by hanging around the chatty Hogan, or perhaps just through sheer repetition of public speaking, Carter would become much more at ease on the microphone. Like the time at a meeting of defense attorneys in Montreal in 2000, just as Denzel Washington's movie portrayal of his life was hitting theaters. That day, Carter led off with a joke about his appearance differing from the movie star's by saying, "For those of you who came here today expecting to see Denzel Washington, I apologize" and then later when speaking about his prison term, adding, "Trenton State Prison was so bad even the cockroaches refused to come in."

Hogan, by comparison, was always gregarious, and it led to him longing to be more a part of the workplace, the adult world, so he left high school, finishing his education at his father's insistence at the Dickinson Evening School while working first at an envelope factory in Jersey City and then as a machinist apprentice in Elizabeth. A desire to explore more of the world led him to take a transfer within that company to Nebraska, where he'd soon realize, "I wasn't really geared toward being a machinist, so I transferred to their foundry smelting bronze and brass and stuff. For about three minutes. It was like 3,000 degrees in there. Had to get out of there."

Seeking more direction, Hogan joined the Army in 1965, his basic training bringing him back to his home state at Fort Dix, the sprawling military base in southern New Jersey that now is part of an even larger complex that includes Army, Air Force and Navy elements. From there, he was sent to Fort Polk, Louisiana, the infamous "Tigerland," whose tropical climate matched what most of those being trained there would face in Vietnam. The word "Vietnam" was just beginning to gain currency in America at that time, and though Hogan's units remained combat-ready, he was lucky enough to miss in-country action in that conflict, instead moving around with a NATO unit through Turkey, Greece and other parts of Europe.

Eventually, his tour of duty ended, and the search for employment that didn't hold the prospect of being sent to Vietnam brought him back to New Jersey and a short stint on the Atlantic Highlands police force. There, he got his first taste of the unrest that would envelop many New Jersey cities in the mid- to late-'60s and early-'70s, being sent to Asbury Park to help quell the riots that beset that bottoming-out resort town. Ironically, it was those types of clashes between police and mainly minority protesters/rioters that would lead Carter to call for residents to take up arms against police.

"Back in our day on the police force," said Ken Grover, Hogan's former police partner, "if you screwed something up, went too far, you'd get time off, whatever. But these days, you go to jail for some of that stuff. I think police are backing away from that kind of confrontation now. It's gotta be a lot more difficult than when we were cops."

Realizing that serving in a very small police department meant that "unless somebody retired or died, I wasn't going to advance very quickly," Hogan responded to a classified ad for investigators in what was then a three-year-old effort to establish a statewide Public Defender Office to coordinate legal defense for the indigent, as mandated by the case of *Gideon v. Wainwright* out of Florida.

It was this job that would put him back into regular contact with the boxer whose sketchy conviction had yet to gain attention outside New Jersey, who was not yet the folk hero of song and literature and film, but whom Hogan felt had been railroaded in a criminal justice system that, at the time, had several sets of rules, one of which was heavily biased against black defendants such as Carter and Artis.

Looking back, Hogan sees where the lessons his parents instilled in him as a youth were at the core of his desire to help Carter and Artis.

"It was a combination of my family background and my professional influences that led me to get involved," he says. "I had an upbringing that taught me if you felt something was wrong, and you could help right it, even if it wasn't the popular thing to do, you had an obligation to correct it.

"Even when I started as a police officer, it wasn't only to enforce the law, but I always felt you had to temper justice with mercy. It was a little different once I got to the public defender's office. When you're representing someone as a defendant, whether you think they're guilty or not, everyone deserves to have their day in court, either in front of a judge or being tried by a jury of their peers. And **they** must find that you're guilty beyond a reasonable doubt.

"No matter who you talked to," Hogan says, looking back, "whether they felt Rubin and John did this or didn't do this, the one thing everyone agrees on is that they didn't get a fair trial. In this country, that should mean that you can't be convicted."

THREE

Seeking Rights for All Inmates While Pursuing Justice for Two of Them

(Late-November/early December 1971: Five-and-a-half years after the Lafayette triple murder)

In the immediate aftermath of the "Rahway Prison Riot" on Thanksgiving 1971, New Jersey Public Defender Stanley Van Ness (who would become a lifelong confidant and mentor) assigned Fred Hogan to the prison to begin documenting inmate complaints about the conditions there. At his side in that effort would be one inmate he already knew quite well, Rubin "Hurricane" Carter.

"3 Wing had movies that night. When I arrived at the auditorium, several individuals (inmates) were already in the process of trying to rile the other inmates to revolt. But this was not a collective feeling upon the totality of the population. In fact, no one knew actually what was taken (sic) place." **– Statement by Rubin "Hurricane" Carter regarding the start of the Rahway riot. November 26, 1971, as recorded in the "inmate grievance ledger" kept by Carter and Fred Hogan.**

The aftermath of the Rahway riot provided yet another opportunity for the bond to grow between Carter, Artis and Hogan. And it was the first glimpse the three would have at the way in which their shared desire to see justice done would impact something broader than the Lafayette Bar and Grille case.

Public Defender Stanley Van Ness, at Hogan's urging, decided to embed his ambitious young investigator at the riot-scarred prison to gather information from inmates that would inform how Van Ness could translate Governor Cahill's promises of reform into actions.

For all their pretense to order and regiment, prisons, especially to the outsider, can be confusing, chaotic places. Two agendas held by two populations – inmates and correctional officials, the latter of which includes the guards – can provide wildly differing accounts of any given event. That gets even trickier when the inmates break off into groups that are largely defined by racial and ethnic lines, where loyalty to the group, and especially to the leaders of the group, becomes far more important than the "truth" of any matter. And that makes getting to the "truth" akin to reaching into a box full of glass shards in hopes of pulling out a diamond.

Hogan was about to find out how much that was the case in the "Thanksgiving Riot" of 1971 at New Jersey Eastern State Penitentiary, colloquially known as "Rahway" or "Rahway Prison." In the riot's aftermath, Hogan was asked by New Jersey Public Defender Stanley Van Ness to set up shop at Rahway and act as the collector of grievances by the inmates so that Governor Cahill's promises of addressing their issues wouldn't go unfulfilled.

Hogan already had become familiar with many inmates at Rahway, some who were Public Defender clients and some, like Rubin Carter and John Artis, who weren't. Almost from the beginning of his tenure with the Office of the Public Defender, Hogan had been visiting Carter, and then Artis, behind Rahway's bars.

"The first time I sought Rubin out, he didn't remember me and, frankly, I didn't expect him to," Hogan says. "So I refreshed his memory about the visit to the training camp and I said, you know, you were kind to me that day, and whatever. He was very quiet. Very hesitant to speak to me, very hesitant. And I said, 'I think you got screwed on your verdict.' Actually, I think the exact words I used were, I think you got **fucked**. I said, 'If an all-white jury found you guilty beyond a reasonable doubt when they were going for the death penalty, there's no way they would come back with a recommendation of mercy (on the sentencing).' That got his attention.

"So I told him I wanted to read more about the case and said I'd be back. And I began to visit him on my own time, on weekends. I was most interested in the fact that they stopped him, John Artis and another guy that night, then let them go. Then they stop Rubin and John again. By this time, the third guy, a guy by the name of John 'Bucks' Royster, had gotten out of the car. They bring them to the scene and nobody could identify them, not even Bello and Bradley."

Bello-and-Bradley. The other names besides Carter-and-Artis that will forever be linked together almost as a single name in the Lafayette case. Small-time hoods not unknown to local law enforcement, they were around the corner from the Lafayette Bar and Grille that night, committing a break-in at the Ace Metal Company.

"Supposedly, they were committing a break-in and Bello hears shots," Hogan says. "He goes to the Lafayette, climbs over the bodies and starts rifling the register. Patricia Graham Valentine, who lived upstairs over the Lafayette, comes down and sees him doing that and he says, 'Oh, I'm just looking for a dime to call the cops.' So the cops pick up Rubin again and bring him to the bar and nobody can identify him, including Bello and Bradley. They take him to the hospital where the surviving gunshot victim is, and Rubin and John are standing at the foot of that guy's bed, and **he** can't identify them. He says, 'No, it's not them.'"

Hogan continued finding time to talk with Carter about the case. The more they spoke, the more Hogan questioned how the Passaic County Prosecutor's Office had maneuvered around Bello and Bradley, using pending charges against them as leverage to coerce statements that the two men knew it was Carter and Artis who had carried out the shootings at the Lafayette. This would later become part of a larger picture of corruption and an anything-for-the-win mentality in that prosecutor's office.

Meanwhile, the regular visits to Carter had, unbeknownst to either man, set the stage for the next chapter in their intertwined lives, which was not directly related to the Lafayette case, but instead was tied to Hogan's key role in the response to the Rahway riot. With Governor Cahill hoping to set New Jersey apart from the Attica fiasco that occurred under Governor (soon to be Vice President) Nelson Rockefeller in New York, and Stanley Van Ness aiming to reform a system of prejudice against indigent defendants and inmates (especially those who were African-American) the riot opened up an opportunity to address the abuses of both the criminal justice system and the prisons.

With Hogan asked to lead the investigatory effort on compiling and documenting inmate grievances, his and Carter's collaboration was about to take on an even larger footprint than solely the Lafayette case.

"I was only about 26 in 1971, and I'm thinking maybe there was a little naivete on my part," Hogan recalls. "I knew enough people there that I felt they would trust me, especially if they were asking for me and asking for some negotiations. I felt that if they really wanted to talk to each other, I'd be able to bridge that gap. But I wasn't stupid enough to say, 'Throw me in, coach.' I could've been seen as another one of these bleeding heart liberals from the outside, what I call the limousine liberals, who show up in their dungarees and tie-dyed shirts and they drop you off around the corner, out of your limousine, and then when it's all over you go back and change into your suit in the limo."

Part of Hogan's confidence came from the high esteem in which he held then-State Public Defender Stanley Van Ness, another man who, much like Carter, would become a lifelong friend, mentor and inspiration for Hogan.

Fred Hogan and Stanley Van Ness

"I guess I felt I could do it because of Stanley Van Ness' insight and the compassion he had for (people facing) all types of injustices. He was just a unique guy. He could walk among all people comfortably. I mean, (Governor) Cahill was a Republican and Stanley was a Democrat. Stanley was black and Cahill was white. You know, Cahill caught a ration of shit for reappointing Stanley (as Public Defender). (Van Ness) was the first person (in New Jersey) to have the insight to at least do something about prison reform and at least start a dialogue about it. Stanley saw that, and he saw something in me. I knew there were things that needed to be discussed (about the prisons). The educational piece, the medical care."

Governor Cahill too, at least publicly, saw the Rahway riot as a call to action on the conditions of New Jersey's prisons, saying in the aftermath of the riots that he recognized conditions in the institutions "definitely" needed immediate reform.

So, in the days immediately following the riot, Hogan, with Van Ness' blessing, began reporting each day to the prison, trying to work with and within an inmate grievance committee that included representation from every wing and, by its nature, the various factions within a prison population that are usually broken down by race, ethnicity and even the type of crime for which one was convicted.

The list of grievances Hogan heard from inmates as he interviewed them separately and in meetings with the inmate grievance committee ranged from a lack of educational opportunities to poor medical care to beatings by guards both before and directly after the riots.

While certainly less stressful than seeing a prison in flames and cops clad in riot gear restlessly waiting outside, getting to the root of what had made inmates want to riot was a more complex task. To be sure, some grievances were more legitimate than others.

"Even before the riots," Hogan said, "when I'd be in the prison visiting our (Public Defender) clients or visiting Rubin, I'd get inmates (saying), 'Hey Hogan, look at this food. This is garbage!' Now, I knew some of the cooks, and I knew it wasn't *that* bad. But there were issues. It was very structured. There was Administrative Segregation, Court Line, taking privileges away. If you even looked sarcastically at an officer, you'd be in trouble. There was no benefit of the doubt."

One complaint involved an inmate named Rosa, who told of being beaten by guards after the riot was quelled because one of them had been cut by flying glass from a bottle thrown by an inmate they believed to be Rosa:

> Inmate Rosa is presently confined in Administrative Segregation, and has filed against (sic) (by the prison authorities) criminal charges of "Assault and Battery" upon an officer.

> Unequivocally, this inmate was beaten. I saw many contusions (black + blue) covering his body...and he appeared to have been physically abused by someone." – **Inmate Grievance Ledger entries of November 26, 1971.**

Fred Hogan reads the Inmate Grievance Ledger he and Rubin "Hurricane" Carter kept in the aftermath of the Rahway riot.

Just as frequently as guards being accused of brutality, however, inmates were complaining about a lack of supervision that led to their being brutalized by other prisoners. Early in the process of listening to grievances by the inmates, Hogan was confronted by a prisoner who reported being raped by five other inmates. Yet, even within the confines of the committee formed to hear grievances, the prisoner would not name his attackers:

> It is my understanding from what this inmate related to me that he plans to seek his own revenge. By this, I take it to mean that this individual might eventually stab the inmates who were directly responsible for these crimes against his person. –**Ledger entry of November 30, 1971.**

Ironically, while rape was rampant in most prisons, sex offenders of all stripes, not just pedophiles, often were targeted for particularly brutal treatment by fellow inmates. This was documented in the wake of the riot as a complaint to Hogan by an inmate named Parker. On December 8, 1971, he described to Hogan an attack during the riot on a "5 Wing" inmate, referring to the wing that at the time housed Rahway's sex offenders. The following was recorded in the ledger, recounting Parker's account of the incident:

> When I arrived there, I saw a group of inmates crowded around a cell getting ready to break the locking devise (sic) off the door. They were trying to get to a 5 Wing inmate named (DELETED), who was locked up inside. (W)hen the lock on the cell door was finally broken, the inmates then surged inside armed with knives and iron pipes. At this point...I intervened and took (the inmate) away from the others and transported him to...safety. – **Ledger entry of December 8, 1971.**

Clearly, the multitude of agendas, grudges, alliances – and mental illness leading to perceived slights that never happened – was going to make organizing the inmates into a cohesive unit to bargain with Governor

Cahill's new Committee on Prison Reform a monumental task. Hogan noted as much in a journal entry early on the process.

I found the Inmate Committee to be very much unorganized and equally confused. – **Ledger entry of December 7, 1971.**

Meetings of the inmate committee often degenerated into debates about procedure or laundry lists of a wing representative's own personal gripes against other inmates, about issues such as who looked at whom the wrong way, instead of focusing on the "original 14" demands that had been compiled by the inmates during the riot. It was like trying to corral a roomful of kindergartners, only these kindergartners could rip your throat out. So getting tough with them wasn't exactly an option. Hogan's own frustrations with the process were recorded in a ledger note:

Yet again today I encountered problems concerning the inmates negotiation committee on grievances. And it seems to me that problems are forever prevailing between the inmates and the inmate committee on grievances. – **Ledger entry of December 13, 1971.**

Hogan even noted in the ledger that he sensed a distrust by the inmates toward himself, even though he was the one they had asked for as a negotiator. This distrust, he felt, was not because of anything about him personally, but because he was employed by the Public Defender's Office, and hence the State.

"My main forte was giving the credibility to the PD's Office, in that we were not 'one of them,' you know, in bed with the prosecutor, the stereotypical stuff that you'd hear inmates say. You know, like, 'You get paid by the same people as the prosecutor. You go to lunch together, you go to conferences together.' A lot of that was just showboating by some inmates. But there's nothing left for you to say. You have to be very careful not to get into defending that and trying to explain what that meant."

While Hogan clearly recognized the inmate committee's shortcomings, he would soon be faced with a greater threat to keeping a lid on the simmering tensions that still lay just beneath the surface in the aftermath of the Thanksgiving riot.

Pressure from the public and media to "do something" about the conditions that had led to the riot was mounting. Governor Cahill, frustrated with the time it was taking for the inmates to reach any consensus on the priority of their issues, moved forward with announcing a prison-reform agenda that pre-empted the inmates.

In a press release dated January 3, 1972, a little over a month after the riot, Cahill said he was "disappointed by the lack of progress in negotiations with prisoners following the Rahway disturbances on Thanksgiving Day," and announced a "series of sweeping reforms for parole, living conditions, health and education for inmates of New Jersey's penal institutions.

"The Governor," the press release continued, "said he had purposely announced the recommendations as the first order of business in 1972 to emphasize the importance of this question of penal reform."

In short, the promise to listen to all of the inmates' concerns had held firm for just over a month before the need to feel like "something" was being done superseded it. As the press release noted, "The conditions call for action, not debate. We intend to proceed immediately."

At an Inmate Grievance Committee meeting that day, at which the committee members were irate over what they saw as Cahill's premature announcement, one inmate was quoted in Hogan's journal as saying, "Because of the Governor's news release, I'm finding an abundance of hostility directed towards the committee members by the general population." In short, the inmates not on the committee assumed those who were a part of it had "sold out" the rest of the population.

Clearly, it wasn't a comfortable time to be a member of the committee. Some inmates even drafted a petition to "impeach" their fellow prisoners on the committee, though Hogan was able to convince the petitioners to withdraw it. In its stead, a group of inmates not on the committee sent a letter to Cahill, dated January 4, 1972, imploring him to focus on a few key issues of health, food, sanitation, parole procedures, disciplinary procedures, work-release issues and racism among certain guards. Ironically, the letter asked that security not be relaxed "to the point where the institution becomes a 'shooting gallery' for the few inmates who would like to do their time in a constant state of euphoria."

Whatever their issues with the inmate committee, these non-committee inmates made it clear that "Mr. Stanley Van Ness and his representative and liaison Mr. Fred Hogan from his office deserve recognition for the selfless manner in which he has attempted to bring these meetings a semblance of organization and sanity."

As a result of the backlash from their fellow inmates, the committee tried putting aside its internal differences and a series of "joint" meetings between representatives from the Governor's Office and the inmate committee was set.

The first steps of what would become a formal, official "Inmate Advocacy" movement in the state of New Jersey had been taken, said Gerald Boswell, a retired New Jersey Office of the Public Defender attorney.

"Stanley (Van Ness) was the one who, once the Department of the Public Advocate was created, made it possible to be able to sue on the part of inmates, and all of that took effect as a direct result of what Stanley, Fred and all those people did at Rahway after the riot."

To be sure, not all of Hogan's colleagues, even some inside the Public Defender's Office, held respect for what Hogan was trying to do, both in prison reform and on the Carter/Artis case.

"Yeah," Hogan recalls, "I used to get anonymous hate mail accusing me of being a 'nigger lover' or threats that 'something bad should happen to you because you believe these murdering niggers.' There were even colleagues in the Public Defender system. Now, they wouldn't come right out with blatant stuff like the hate mail did, but you'd get the looks, the comments. Things like, 'Do you *really* think these guys are innocent?'

"Well, in the Public Defender system, you know you've represented people we knew, deep down, were guilty. But you can't be a hypocrite about it. But that doesn't mean you don't take it personally when someone says something or writes you a letter. When I think about what it would've been like today, with e-mail and Facebook and Twitter and all of that out there, it would've been a bombardment of negativity and accusations."

FOUR

"Scared Straight" emerges in the Rahway riot's aftermath

(Mid-1976:About 10 years after the Lafayette triple murder)

For the most part, John Artis kept a much more low-key role in prison than did his co-defendant Rubin Carter. While Carter was helping Hogan make sense of the various inmate grievances that were at the heart of the prison-reform movement, Artis busied himself with the things that had occupied him before he was locked up, namely athletics, participating prison baseball, football and basketball programs. The one exception was his involvement in the "Lifers" group, which ultimately would spark a famous effort to try to steer youth away from crime.

Some of the justice-system impacts that the Carter-Artis-Hogan connection would bring about are familiar to people of certain generations, although even those people may not know that the trio's interactions had a role in their formation.

One of those innovations in the system would become, first, a highly regarded, then later a hotly debated, attempt to have inmates play a pivotal part in trying to keep youngsters from following in the inmates' path.

Hogan and Carter's recording of inmate grievances would serve not only as a release valve for inmates to talk about troubling violence between inmates and guards (as well as among the inmates themselves) but also as a catalyst for prisoners to begin discussing how they would like to address their image while also potentially "giving something back to the community" for the crimes that led to their sentences.

This was of particular interest to those serving life behind bars, or at least a sentence of 25 years or longer. Knowing that they were likely to never again have any identity than that of an inmate, or at best an "ex-con," they began discussing the idea of a group that could talk to troubled youth about the dangers of continuing down a wrong path. That effort soon came to be known as "The Lifers' Group," and then later, thanks to media exposure, as "Scared Straight."

According to James Finckenauer in his 1982 book "Scared Straight! and the Panacea Phenomenon," the Lifers' Group "was created in part to counteract what these inmates saw as a stereotyped, Hollywood-type image of prisons and convicts held by the general public. This image, they felt, stigmatized convicts as immoral and inhuman. In order to dispel what they saw as a false image, the Lifers wanted to try to prove that they could be useful and worthwhile people even though locked up in a maximum-security prison."

The president of the group was Richard Rowe, who, according to numerous articles of that time, felt personally invested in the approach because he had a 12-year-old son whom he did not want to see follow in his footsteps. A short time later, John Artis would become the Vice President of the group.

Rowe was able to push the idea forward, Artis said, because, "he had some connections, some inroads, to certain judges and stuff in various counties. We brainstormed and we came up with this idea to give something back to the community, to have kids and college students come in and get a bird's eye view of what life was like in the prison.

"When we would talk to the kids, it was basically, 'If you don't cut out what you're doing, you can wind up here.' The one judge that Rowe knew, he took that and started where, as part of the sentence he would give in Juvenile Court, he was making it mandatory that they come to this Juvenile Awareness Program. That's what we called it, not 'Scared Straight.' That (title) came later from the TV shows about it. So that started to circulate, some newspaper stories were written and it got on TV, and then other judges started sending kids there. Then social workers got involved bringing kids in, and probation officers, college professors. All kinds of people started getting involved."

The program picked up steam quickly, and it went from a once-a-week schedule to two groups of juveniles a day being brought to the prison. Television specials detailing the program in 1978 made the methods well-known and, ironically, both praised and controversial at the same time.

The scenes from those shows are familiar to anyone who was in their teens or older in the late-'70s. Juveniles would be brought into the prison, instructed to relinquish their shoes, and seated before a group of inmates at the front of the room.

One by one, the Lifers would relate the realities of daily prison life in highly graphic, often expletive-laden terms. Lifers would first read from newspaper clippings about their own crimes, partly to establish them as people the juveniles did not want to mess with. Others would read articles about prisoners who were killed while serving time, often "short-timers" who were killed by more dangerous inmates over things such as "a picture of his woman that he had in his cell that another sick motherf---er wanted and killed him for."

Juveniles who either smiled or were noted as not paying attention to the inmates' liking were singled out for individual verbal abuse, often at nose-to-nose range, with the inmate yelling as loudly as possible. Some saw their shoes flung to the far side of the room. Some would even be chased from the room if a Lifer took a particular disliking to them.

With national attention focused on the effort, and with initial reports touting it as highly successful in steering troubled youth away from a life of crime, prisons throughout the nation began employing similar programs.

"We felt good about what we were doing," Artis said. "It wasn't any powderpuff kind of deal. We weren't sugar-coating anything. We just said, this is what it *will* be like if you're a kid and you're coming in here with real-life criminals."

Eventually, and maybe inevitably, enough youngsters who had gone through the program committed more serious crimes as adults, and critics would seize upon those statistics to declare it a failure. No one knows how many of the youngsters didn't commit additional crimes because of their prison visits and went on to lead quiet, law-abiding lives. The criminal-justice system doesn't keep those kinds of statistics.

Though Artis believes there were some kids the program certainly reached, he ultimately reached the conclusion that 90 minutes locked away, even with the most hardened criminals, just wasn't long enough.

"You can't literally *scare* anybody straight," he said. "An hour and a half with us and then you go right back out to free society… It puts fear in them while they're there, but…

"The most important thing, we felt, was trying to make these kids aware of where or what could happen with the negative behavior they were engaging in, like stealing or fighting in school, and instead trying to push them toward some positive stuff. The inmates used examples of their own lives, saying, 'Yeah, I did just what you are doing when I was your age, and look where I am now. And if you don't stop, I'll be waiting for ya when you get here.'"

The creation of the Lifers' Group and "Scared Straight" is indicative of the approach both Carter and Artis (and Hogan, as well) often took in wanting to do what they can to steer juveniles, and at time adults, away from any way of life that would wind them up behind bars.

One such occasion was in November 2004, when Carter addressed the young residents of the New Jersey State Home for Boys, a.k.a. "Jamesburg," the very institution he called home for so many years of his youth. A final draft of that speech is among the thousands of documents recently collected by Tufts University to set up the Dr. Rubin Carter Archives, which is dedicated to preserving the records of the Carter/Artis case, as well as voluminous writings by Carter that dealt with the case and its aftermath right up to his death from cancer in 2014.

In stark contrast to the in-your-face tone that many of the *Scared Straight!* inmates set when at-risk youth visited them, Carter's tone in the speech is more like a father talking to his children in a way that encourages them to change their path, but without the extreme tactics used in *Scared Straight!*

In the speech, Carter tells a story of a busy father who wants to "buy some time" before playing with his son. So he tears a map of the world out of a newspaper article, breaks it into many pieces, and then tells the son he will play with him once the son has reassembled the map. Within five minutes, though, the boy was back with the completed picture, to his father's astonishment.

"'How did you do that so quickly?' the father asked," Carter said. "The little boy looked up innocently...'Daddy,' he said, 'on the front of the page that you gave me...was a map of the world...but on the other side, there was a picture of a little boy. So I just put the boy back to-gether…and when I turned the page over…the world was all together, too.'

"It is you…and you…and you…each one of you," Carter continued. "When you come together, you make the world come together…and when YOU change, the world around you changes. In fact, that is the only way the world changes."

Though certainly not to the shock-value level of Scared Straight, Carter did try to impress upon the inhabitants of his former home the reali-ties of prison life.

"During my twenty-plus years in adult prison, I learned that prison is the lowest level of human existence," he said. "The best you can expect is for someone to allow you to wear your own clothes or someone to allow you to watch television or whatever else. But you usually can't make those decisions for yourself. Someone else does."

FIVE

New Jersey's Inmate Advocacy Rises from the Repercussions of Rahway

(Late-1971/early-1972: Five to six years after the Lafayette triple murder)

"You can judge a society by the way it treats its prisoners" - Winston Churchill

"The degree of civilization in a society can be judged by entering its prisons." – Fyodor Dostoyevsky

Multiple variations of those two quotes have been attributed to Gandhi, President Harry Truman, Pope John Paul II and others. Sometimes "prisoners" or "prisons" is replaced by "minorities," "the poor," or "children and the elderly," but the sentiment is essentially the same – how well the rights of the vulnerable, or the outcasts of society, are protected speaks volumes to that society's values.

That sentiment was and often remains at the heart of the message when the principals in the Lafayette Bar and Grille case discuss the tortuous road Carter and Artis were forced to travel as they proclaimed their innocence. Even today, when Hogan and Artis collectively or singularly speak to students, exoneration activists and others about the case and its impact on criminal justice, that theme will emerge.

The original intent of those quotes at the start of this chapter was clearly on the mind of then-Public Defender Stanley C. Van Ness in the wake of the Rahway riot of 1971. He made it clear to Fred Hogan, who had enlisted the aid of Rubin "Hurricane" Carter in documenting inmate grievances leading up to the riot, that bringing a new era of civility to New Jersey's prisons was not only a benefit for those behind bars, but also important to avoid an Attica-style rampage in the state's major lock-ups that could cost lives or millions of taxpayer dollars.

In early-December 1971, in the wake of the riot, visits to inmates had been suspended and they were being kept in their cells around the clock, leading Hogan to record in the journal on Saturday, December 11, 1971:

> Not withstanding the tensions of the riot itself, the moral(e) factors
> of the inmates of Rahway State Prison are exceedingly low. Due
> to the fact, I suspect, of missing their weekly visits and...having to
> remain locked in their cells for 24 hours a day.

A bit of a turning point came when Hogan and the then-acting superintendent negotiated a reinstatement of the inmate visits. This not only acted as a release valve for some of the pressure building up in the inmates, but helped to get the members of the Grievance Committee to put more trust in what Hogan, Van Ness and Carter were doing. (Although, as mentioned previously, the rush by Governor Cahill to make a press splash with proposed reforms would bring those feelings of distrust to a boil once again.)

Pressure was building on Hogan, not only from the inmates, but from the prison administration, as noted in the following journal entry from Tuesday, December 21, 1971:

It is my impression (that) the prison administration has never before been questioned – or ever asked – to clarify or verify any actions or statements made by them in the past. And now, with my presence in and about the prison daily, asking via the inmates' requests for simple and logical answers – the powers to be here at Rahway feel that I am a threat to their long-established and never-before-questioned policies.

What neither Hogan nor Carter fully realized at the time was that they were laying the groundwork for what would later become an institutionalized part of the New Jersey Department of the Public Advocate, namely the Division of Inmate Advocacy. The broader department also would encompass the Office of the Public Defender, as well as a division devoted to providing representation for the mentally ill, a Law Guardian unit to provide attorneys to fight for children in abuse cases, and several programs aimed at protecting consumers, such as enforcing new-home warranties and fighting against unreasonable rate increases by public utilities.

"Inmate Advocacy was never officially under the Public Defender," Hogan says. "Stanley (Van Ness) reached beyond what the Public Defender did because most of the people were our clients, and were on appeal So Stanley made the case that there should be a Public Advocate, and then the Public Defender became part of the Department of the Public Advocate. It was very positive and productive under Stanley. But then it got watered down with the Public Advocates after him because they did not have the unique ability to do what Stanley did."

It strikes one to think how bold and ahead-of-the-curve it was for Van Ness, Hogan and other key players in the Office of the Public Defender to decide to devote resources to standing up for basic human rights in prison. This was the age of Nixon, Kent State, race riots, anti-hippie sentiment, Vietnam. Most of the people in positions of power, who had come of age in the late-'40s and 1950s, had little sympathy for those convicted and sentenced to prison, especially if those prisoners happened to be minorities.

Arthur Penn was an integral player in the work of the Department at that time. His recollection of the Rahway riot of Thanksgiving 1971 is much like Fred Hogan's – chaotic, filled with potential death and disaster, and, ultimately, cleansing and beneficial for New Jersey's prison system. He also gives a lot of credit for the riot not becoming a repeat of the Attica-style carnage to two men – then-Governor William Cahill and Rubin "Hurricane" Carter.

"It was such a frightening scene when we got there," recalls Penn, who spent 22 years (1969-1981) in the New Jersey Office of the Public Defender and Department of Public Advocate before retiring and entering private practice. "The troopers were marching in the parking lot as a show of force. When we went in, the prison was so full of troopers that you had to walk single file to get through them all. That's all the room you had."

Initially, Penn was fearful about the outcome. Certainly, from all indications, the two sides were preparing to dig in for a confrontation, and a bloody one, if need be.

"The warden, he was a tough mother," Penn says, "and he thought he was just going to go into this thing with a hundred drunk, rioting inmates, with just **one** guard with him, and just tell them that that's it, this was over, go back to their cells.

"That was when they took him hostage."

What Penn was unaware of until later in the crisis was that Governor Cahill had decided early on to avoid an Attica replay at all costs, and that emphasizing the demands of the inmates was a cornerstone of that approach.

"Governor Cahill did a magnificent job; he certainly was instrumental in saving the day," Penn says. "You could tell he was really interested in terms of hearing the prisoners' grievances and in bringing real reform to the prisons. And I think THAT, right on that day, was the real start of recognizing that inmates do have rights, that they are human beings, and that they should be treated fairly. That was the start of Inmate Advocacy."

Ironically, Penn said, the ensuing days brought to light that any systematic approach to inmate grievances was not really what sparked the Rahway riot, and that the inmates needed to begin couching their accounts of the riot as if it had been.

"It was my impression that the prison riot, in terms of the inmates actually deciding to riot, had little if anything to do with prison reform," he says. "Basically, it was Thanksgiving, they were drunk and feeling riled up."

Fred Hogan and Art Penn

It was in that sense, Penn believes, that Rubin Carter, and to some degree John Artis, played such a crucial role – keeping a clear head when the combination of (in Hogan's words) "jailhouse hooch," frustration, a police response mounting outside and ongoing inmate grievances (against authorities and each other) were causing many inmates to lose their cool.

"Rubin did have a very calming effect on the inmates during the riot," says Penn. "They respected him, so when he said to go back to their cells, get water, those kinds of things, they listened to him. And he and John Artis, from what I've been told, did a lot to keep guards safe and discourage inmates from hurting guards or taking hostages. They were urging people not to get involved in that way."

While the inmates may not have had a concept of their actions being aimed at prison reform, the riot *was* the catalyst for both sides to start talking about making changes inside the institution.

"There were a lot of legitimate grievances that the inmates had," Penn says, "and I remember us saying to them, 'You have to stick to talking about the legitimate reasons as to why you were rioting.' Because, at that point, the administration was very open to doing something. And it wasn't like they had a lot of choice, because this was right after Attica. It was more a matter of either go in and shoot a lot of people, or figure out something else to do."

To be sure, though, there wasn't a complete "forgive-and-forget" approach by law enforcement in the wake of the riot.

"There were trials after the riot, where inmates were charged," Penn recalls, "and I represented one of the inmates, a guy named Dusty Anderson. When he went to trial, we emphasized that he was hiding the warden in his cell, and the jury acquitted him. I remember Dusty's case especially. They wanted to give him 30 additional years for his involvement in the riot. Now, some of these guys were, in fact, deeply involved, but Dusty wasn't one of them. He was very concerned he was going to wind up with 30 years, minimum (added to his sentence).

There were a lot of people in that prison who were looking to riot. But there were some who did a lot to calm things down."

Art Penn

While Penn's involvement in inmate advocacy issues was focused on the immediate aftermath of the riot, it would be up to another Hogan acquaintance, Arnold Mellk, to pick up the long-term cause for the inhabitants of New Jersey's prisons. From the point about a week after the Rahway riot and for a six-year period, Mellk was the New Jersey Department of the Public Advocate's Office of Inmate Advocacy legal representative in Stanley Van Ness' new effort to ensure that prisoners were treated with at least the basics of human dignity.

As the choice of Van Ness to be the lead counsel in the new Inmate Advocacy efforts, Mellk found unwanted attention paid to him by the authorities.

"In that role, I had to go to the prisons all the time," he says. "The FBI started following me. They thought I was like the consigliere for the African-American prisoners. People were sitting out in front of my home. I used to stop these guys, and I'd say, 'I just got back from Vietnam. Where'd you serve?'

"But I never, **ever** got any interference from Governor Cahill, either himself or the attorney general for Cahill. I can't say the same for the next group that came in, for Governor (Brendan) Byrne's people. He (Byrne) was OK, but his people weren't nearly as cooperative as Cahill's administration when it came to what we were doing.

"I'd even get calls from my father. He'd say, 'Didn't I teach you better?'"

What many in the penal system didn't understand at the time, Mellk says, is that advocating for better treatment of inmates creates, by extension, a safer environment for corrections officers and others working in the prison.

As in many issues, pendulums swing back, and the "war on drugs" created a new sense of antagonism from the public toward inmates. Like many involved in the criminal justice system, Mellk sees the drug war as a broken approach that unfairly targets minorities and serves only to fill prisons with people who would be better off in treatment facilities.

Arnold Mellk and Fred Hogan

"Forty percent of people who are in prison are there because of drugs and drug use," he says. "A lot of issues arise out of how you are brought up. If your environment is one of poverty and violence, chances are that is how you will act. We've got to get back into the communities."

These days, as a private-practice attorney, Mellk concentrates on civil rights cases, including what he sees as child-welfare authorities abusing their power. But he looks back proudly on his days spent trying to "change the culture" of what it meant to be an inmate through the involvement of the Inmate Advocacy Unit, which was yet another outgrowth of the efforts of Hogan, Carter and Artis.

"We were dealing with the most despised among us," Mellk says. "But the mark of a civilization is how you treat those people."

SIX

"The Lover," "The Other Guy," "Basketball John"

(Late-1974: About eight years after the Lafayette triple murder)

While he is often referred to as "the other guy" or "the forgotten man" in the saga of the triple murder at the Lafayette Bar and Grille, John Artis was as much a wrongfully convicted man as was Rubin Carter. And he often has played as much a pivotal role in the post-prison efforts to draw attention to ongoing inequities in the justice system as have Hogan and Carter.

If Carter was the high-profile boxer who had already become known by the time the two men were arrested and charged, Artis was the talented high-school athlete (track, especially) who never really got started chasing his dreams of athletic fame and fortune.

Arrested at the age of 19 in the Lafayette case, Artis did 15 years, in New Jersey's state prison system before being paroled ("5,478 days," he says, still mindful of every turn of the calendar page). Unlike his co-defendant, he had no history of run-ins with the law as a juvenile, no history of any kind with the type of incendiary comments

Carter had made about police and their relationship to the black community.

John Artis

Artis, in fact, was already out of prison on parole when the federal court decision overturning his and Carter's convictions was rendered. But not for the reasons prosecutors wanted, as illustrated by an encounter in late-1974.

"They came to me over and over again, saying, 'Just say Carter did it and you'll walk out of here,'" Artis recalls. "That started during the investigation and continued after we went to prison. I wasn't going to say that, because it wasn't true. At one point, I ended up down in Leesburg on the prison farm. I had gotten enrolled in some college classes (through a prison program). I had been in prison about six to eight years at that point. And one day I was getting ready to go to class and they came and said, 'C'mon, you're going to Paterson.' I said, 'But I have to go to classes.' They said, 'Not today. You have a furlough. You're going to your father's house in Paterson.'

"I hadn't been there to my father's house in eight years. We walk in the door and there's the Assemblyman for the area, Eldridge Hawkins. (Carter case attorney) Lew Steel was there. My parents were there. And the prosecutor was there. He said, 'We know you didn't kill anyone. But we think you were there and we think you know something about it. You sign this statement, saying Rubin Carter did this and you were there. We'll have you out before Christmas.'

"I said, 'No, I'm not doing that, man. Why don't you give lie detector tests to your star witnesses?' I turned and told the (corrections) officer, 'You made me miss classes for **this**? Take me back to Leesburg.'"

Carter, in a speech to a defense attorneys' group in Montreal in 2000, recounted the many times Artis was pressured to give up his co-defendant, ending that portion of his remarks by simply stating, "John Artis is MY hero."

Carter, who'd had infinitely more experience in the penal system, probably anticipated the attempts by prosecutors to turn Artis into a jailhouse snitch when they were sent away for the murders.

"Rubin said to me, in 1970, I think, 'You do what you do, and I'll worry about getting us out of here.' So, I played football, basketball, baseball. I was an athlete, so I was doing what came naturally to me. It also put me a cut above these other (inmates). They had no idea of my talent. I was a former high-school track star. They couldn't outrun me and they couldn't catch me. They nicknamed me 'Radar,' 'cause I was running down balls like Willie Mays. In football, they called me 'Crazy Legs,' like Crazy Legs Hirsch.

His refusal to flip on Carter and take the easy way out, Artis says now, stemmed from a traditional upbringing in rural Virginia that stressed honesty, among other virtues.

"I am a Southerner, and I was born during the era of segregation," he says. "So a black family stuck together back then, especially in Virginia. I had that old-world, old-school country upbringing. 'Yes mam, No mam, Please, Thank you.' My mother was the architect of my life. I had a real strong work ethic instilled in me from an early age. She made me very responsible. Even after we moved to New Jersey, in summers, you were shipped back to Virginia to work with family members on a farm.

John Artis looks at a display in Fred Hogan's home of articles and memorabilia about Rubin Carter and the Carter/Artis case

"It was all those things that I was raised up in that wouldn't let me lie and say Rubin had done it. I think for Rubin, it was my integrity, that even at the risk of facing the electric chair, I wasn't willing to sacrifice him to save myself with a lie. That was the glue that bound us together."

By this time in their prison stretches, Fred Hogan had made his initial outreach to Carter, and the boxer had in turn talked to Artis about meeting with the investigator who wanted to prove their innocence, or, at the very least, that they hadn't received a fair trial. To put it mildly, Artis had his doubts about why this ex-policeman wanted to get involved.

"When Fred first started coming around, we were looking at him like he had four heads," Artis recalls. "He went into that machine-gun rap of his, talking real fast. Nobody else had bothered to communicate or come to see us. We were extremely leery of him, especially because he had been a cop. So we were very guarded in the beginning."

But, in what would later become a hallmark of his career in the Public Defender's Office, Hogan gained Carter and Artis' trust by doing one simple thing – delivering on what he said he would do.

"When somebody says, 'OK, I'm going to do this, that and the other,' and then he actually **does** those things, then you start to trust him," Artis says. "And it wasn't just us. Fred had spent so much time at the prison after the riot, it got to the point where pretty much the whole prison trusted him. Guys would talk to him, and he'd say, 'OK, let me see what I can do,' and then he actually got back to guys and told them where things stood. Trust is a difficult thing to earn from a prisoner, especially if you're from, quote-unquote, the authorities."

In a fairly short time, Hogan began to make things happen for Carter and Artis.

"He said, 'I'm gonna see if I can get two attorneys for you,' and then he got two attorneys for us, Jack Noonan and Paul Feldman. And then he said, "I'm gonna find (star prosecution witnesses) Bello and Bradley and

I'm gonna talk to them.' And then he went and got their statements, the recantations. It put a spark into our hope, that this might be the big piece of the puzzle. In less than a year since this guy first showed up, all these things started happening."

Artis was so impressed by the fast pace of developments once Hogan, Noonan, Feldman and the Office of the Public Defender became involved, that he felt strongly that he and Carter should stick with the OPD in handling their appeals in the case. That led to something of a showdown between them, as Carter believed higher-powered New York City lawyers were the way to go.

"I really wanted to stay with the Public Defender's Office, but Rubin had different ideas," Artis recalls. "And with Rubin, he had that attitude of 'You're either entirely with me or you're against me.' So I just said, 'If that's what you think is best, then OK.' So with some degree of trepidation and discomfort, I went along with that."

Artis, along with many others involved in the case, still sees that decision by Carter as a tactical error. While the New York-based attorneys may have had more resources at their disposal than New Jersey's public defenders, there was, in Artis' view and those of others, a sense throughout the courtroom at the re-trial that the interlopers from New York were not welcome.

"I think everyone, even the jury, kind of had this idea like, 'Who are you to come into New Jersey and tell us what's what?'" Hogan recalls.

Whether that bias against big-city lawyers played a role, or whether the jury weighed Bello and Bradley's recantations against those of some of Carter's alibi witnesses, some of whom also testified at the retrial that they had been less than truthful in their initial statements, the jury in the second trial also found Carter and Artis guilty.

Artis, to say the least, was stunned.

"Couldn't believe it; just couldn't believe it," Artis says. "First, we never fit the description (given of the shooters by several witnesses), and the only commonality we had with them was that we were Afro-American. The description was 'Two tall, light-skinned Negroes, six feet to six-feet-one, 180 to 200 pounds.' Well, Rubin was only about five-foot-eight. He would've had to have been a little porker to be 180 to 200 pounds. On top of that, Bello said he was 10 to 15 feet away from me and that he outran me for about 100 to 150 feet. My high school track coach got on the stand (in the first trial) and said, 'Artis could've given him 99 yards in a 100-yard dash and still caught up to him.'"

As there was between Carter and Hogan, Artis formed unbreakable bonds with both men who would play such pivotal roles in his life. Over the years, Hogan has dubbed Artis "Basketball John," for his athletic prowess and "The Lover," for his reputation as a ladies man.

When Artis was the first inmate allowed outside the prison on a supervised furlough, Hogan was his chaperon. When Artis was married in a jailhouse ceremony, Hogan was his best man. And when Carter became severely ill in June 2011, it was Hogan who went to Toronto to navigate the labyrinth of Canada's socialized medicine system and get him into a hospital. When the cancer growing inside Carter began to take over in the latter part of 2011, Artis went to Toronto to stay with him, to the bitter end, three years later.

When Tufts University established a center at its school of philosophy dedicated to the Carter/Artis case, and invited Artis to receive its Dr. Jean Mayer Global Citizenship Award for both himself and, posthumously, for Carter, he asked Hogan to deliver remarks about the relationship the three men have shared that was born of the fires of the murder case.

Fred Hogan, John Artis, Erin Kelly and Thom Kidrin look at documents in Tufts University's Rubin Carter Archives.

Such was the close link among the three that Hogan was given the "honorary" prison number of 45472½, directly between Carter's 45472 and Artis' 45473. It was to Artis that Carter left instructions to make sure that Hogan, upon Carter's death, received the boxer's prosthetic eye and some of the ashes from his cremation.

"Over the years," Hogan said as part of those remarks made at Tufts, "that friendship has led to many an adventure, as the three of us worked together, and separately, to help others who have been wrongfully convicted."

While Hogan had less than a decade of experience in the criminal justice system when he took up the Carter/Artis case, today he still does not think you had to be a Harvard-educated scholar to see the two men were framed.

"It was the inconsistencies from the very beginning," Hogan says. "Letting them go after what they later claimed was him failing a lie detector test, the lack of physical evidence. Facts are facts, and these were inconsistent with the guilty verdict. When they got arrested, the physical descriptions (of the shooters) were inconsistent with John and Rubin. Four months later, they get re-arrested? It was all because the police got the statements they wanted out of Bello and Bradley. That's when they took the position, all of a sudden, that Rubin had failed the lie detector test. If that's true, then why was he released? You need to have an answer for that."

When Hogan and Artis get together these days, there is still the easy camaraderie that has developed over nearly 50 years of fighting these battles together. It evokes images of Sinatra and Dean Martin, with Hogan ever the fast-talker and Artis' good-humored retorts still carrying a hint of a southern accent. As they prepared to attend a recent event honoring the founder of Centurion Ministries and the 57 people that organization has helped exonerate over the past 35 years, Hogan peppered Artis with suggestion after suggestion about his attire for the day, at one point eliciting a mock-exasperated "Yesssss, Motherrrrrr" from Artis.

Artis helped the people at Tufts sift through the voluminous files, documents, photos and other pieces of Carter's life and legacy for inclusion in the new center there devoted to the case and their work on behalf of others wrongfully convicted.

"Rubin and I will always be joined at the hip, I suppose," he says.

And there isn't a hint of regret in that statement.

Throughout his career, Hogan's work and advocacy led to connections with various high-profile people. Here he is seen with Senator Bill Bradley, on whose presidential campaign Hogan worked.

At a conference on the death penalty, Hogan chats with Sister Helen Prejean of "Dead Man Walking" fame.

SEVEN

The Investigator Becomes Entangled in the Legal System

(Various times between 1966 and 1984)

Throwing oneself into a racially charged, politically heated case in the criminal justice system can have its consequences, even for those not actually charged in the crime. Fred Hogan was about to find that out as his role in the Carter-Artis case became perilous for him as well.

The Hogan-Carter-Artis connection in the justice system was certainly no one-way street. Hogan and his various lawyer acquaintances focused their work on clearing Carter and Artis. Simultaneously, Hogan found himself at least three times on the other end of tough questioning by prosecutors determined to make the Carter-Artis verdicts stand.

Hogan found himself in that position the first time when he obtained the recantations of Bello and Bradley and spurred hearings to get a re-trial for Carter and Artis. To understand the intensity with which prosecutors fought to quell the growing call for a re-trial based on those recantations, it is important to note how unlikely those who prosecuted the case must have thought any such back-tracking by Bello and Bradley would be.

"On the night of the shootings, Patricia Valentine was upstairs (above the Lafayette Bar and Grille) and heard the shots," Hogan says. "She comes down and Bello was rifling the cash register and he says, 'Oh, I was just getting a dime to call the cops.'

"So then the cops came. They had (earlier) stopped Rubin and John, let them go, and then they stopped them again and brought them to the scene. And **nobody** identified them, including Bello and Bradley, who were there.

"So then they take both John and Rubin to the hospital, where the one gunshot victim was still alive, and they bring them to the foot of his bed and **he** did not identify them as the shooters either!"

A few months later, however, both Bello and Bradley had given statements that Carter and Artis **were** the shooters. Armed with those statements of two "eyewitnesses," prosecutors obtained indictments on Carter and Artis.

"A first grand jury didn't indict them," Hogan says, "but with these two statements, from Bello and Bradley, which were the **only** difference in the two grand juries, this second grand jury indicts them."

What wasn't made known to the grand jury or the jury in Carter and Artis' first trial was a tape held by the Passaic County Prosecutor's Office that clearly had a detective from that prosecutor's office promising Bradley help with his ongoing criminal cases.

"Bello and Bradley had been arrested on other crimes in Passaic County," Hogan said, "and on the tape Bradley is told that, 'We know you saw Rubin Carter commit that crime, isn't that right? Now, I can't promise you anything, but I can promise you this...'"

When Hogan sought out both Bello and Bradley in his investigation of the case, he recalls, Bello told him that he'd been promised a reward in the case but had never been paid.

"I found Bello, who at the time was in the Bergen County Jail, and he was the first one who recanted," Hogan says. "He was absolutely pissed that he didn't get the reward money. He kept applying for it and they never gave it to him. They told him he couldn't have it because the case was on appeal. It was a $10,500 reward. And so he was really pissed. So I said, listen, I don't want you to recant because you're pissed, I want you to recant because it's the truth. You lied then and you're telling the truth now."

Fred Hogan in the 1970s

Hogan left the jail that day with Bello's recantation statement. It took him a little longer to track down Bradley.

"I sought Bradley out. He was at his mother's house, in Passaic. He was not to happy to see me. He says, 'What the fuck do you want?' He had a baseball bat, and it just was not a pleasant first meeting."

It took a couple meetings arranged through inmates Hogan had talked to who knew Bradley before he, too, recanted his earlier statement that it was Carter and Artis who committed the murders..

"He said, 'I never really was told about the reward. I was just not taken care of in my cases the way I was promised by the Prosecutor's Office. They said I'd be taken care of on some other trouble.' So, he recanted. I introduced him to John Flynn, an attorney who was helping with the case, and he talked to John and acknowledged his recantation, felt a lot better about it and he did it because promises were given to him that weren't kept. That was the beginning of the grounds for the recantation hearings."

While the recantations were crucial to convincing a higher court to grant a re-trial, they may not have been enough on their own, had there not been a chance meeting between John Noonan, (one of Carter's lawyers and later a federal judge) and a retired detective, who let slip that tapes did indeed exist of the interview in which Bradley was promised certain considerations in exchange for "eyewitness" statements.

Judge Jack Noonan (ret.) and Fred Hogan

"So Noonan said, 'There was nothing in discovery (in the first trial) about a tape about promises, so when we went to court, Noonan put in his discovery papers and seeking these tapes ," Hogan says. "We had to go back in front of Sam Larner, who was the judge in the first trial, and the judge said, 'I presided over this case, and there was never any tapes of witnesses Bello and Bradley.'

"Noonan says, 'Yes there was.' He just took a shot, because that's what this (retired detective) had told him. And the judge says again, 'I presided over this case and there were no such tapes. Mr. Prosecutor, isn't that correct?' And the prosecutor said, 'No judge, that's not correct, there are tapes.' Larner immediately took a recess."

Judge Larner's rejection of the request for a new trial was argued up to the New Jersey Supreme Court before Carter and Artis would be afforded a re-trial. Armed now with the recantations and the knowledge that evidence had been withheld during the first trial, the team representing Carter and Artis felt they had a good shot of securing an acquittal in the retrial. But things were not to go exactly as they planned. And Hogan was about to go from crusading investigator to accused manipulator by prosecutors.

In order to rebut the recantation statements, prosecutors decided to attack the way in which they were obtained. Their theory boiled down to this: Hogan had been named by Carter as an "agent" to receive a $10,000 advance from a publisher on Carter's first prison-penned book, *The 16th Round*. Hogan and Carter maintained that was done because Carter trusted Hogan to give that money to Carter's wife, who could not claim it as income for fear of being thrown off the welfare roles. So, there was never evidence of her actually receiving the money from Hogan.

Prosecutors, in trying to cast the money as a payoff to Bello and Bradley, claimed the money had instead gone to them to "buy" their recantations.

"So when I testified about getting the recantations, they did a pretty good dance on me," Hogan recalls. "There was an attorney, Ron Marmo, who later became a judge, who did an outstanding job of cross-examining me."

It did not help that by the time of the retrial, Bello had recanted his recantation, and had gone back to his original statement from the first trial. This was also the time in which celebrities began rallying behind Carter, and the boxer decided that he should replace the New Jersey lawyers with more high-profile counsel from New York City. It would come to be regarded by many involved in the case as a crucial miscalculation on Carter's part.

"I said to Rubin, 'Listen, it's your decision. You rise and fall on it when you go to court,'" Hogan says. "Rubin said, 'Can you take a leave of absence and still work on the case?' And I said, 'No, I can't, because the New York people are gonna knock the shit out of what the (New Jersey) Public Defender did, and that's what they're supposed to do. And I can't be on a leave of absence and expect to go back after I've just finished flip-flopping on what my agency did.'"

John Flynn, a New Jersey attorney Hogan had encouraged to help in the fight for Carter and Artis, recalls trying to convince Carter that he and other New Jersey lawyers knowing the lay of the land of "Jersey justice" was more important than the pedigrees of the New York attorneys.

"By this time, all the celebrities were involved," Flynn says. "They were having the (fund-raising event) thing over in Madison Square Garden and we were seen as just the local yokels. I remember talking to Rubin years later. He acknowledged that he kinda screwed it up."

Hogan reflects back now with pride on his handling of the tough questioning about the way in which he obtained the recantations and the notes he kept about those conversations. His experience in both law enforcement and criminal defense, as well as the street smarts ingrained in his Jersey City youth, led him to carefully consider how each question was asked and to answer only as it applied to the question.

During an interview at his home, attorney and longtime Hogan friend Frank DeSevo recounted how he was not exactly brimming with confidence when his client showed up to be taken to a deposition.

Frank DeSevo

(Hogan, a drug- and alcohol-abuse counselor who has not had a drink since February 1982, is always candid about his past problems with alcohol and takes a keen interest in helping others facing similar problems. He recently served as president of New Jersey's Lawyers Concerned for Lawyers, a group that helps attorneys with drug- and alcohol-abuse and related issues. He was the first non-lawyer to fill that post. Since 2016, he also has been President of the Council on Compulsive Gambling of New Jersey.)

"You came over here at 6 or 7 in the morning with Jack Noonan," DeSevo said to Hogan, both of them laughing at the memory, "and at that time you were drinking that fire water. I remember you coming in with the drinks. 'Portable breakfast!' They're half in the bag and I'm thinking, 'Oh this is gonna be nice.' They were putting heat on you for months. Talking about aiding and abetting a welfare fraud. They were saying you took money to pay Bello to recant his statement. They didn't care exactly how they disparaged you. 'A' was as good as 'B,' from their point of view, because they wanted you not to testify at the second trial."

Robert DeGroot, a Newark-based attorney who helped Hogan with the Carter/Artis case, said the tactics employed in trying to discredit Hogan and his work to obtain the recantations were part of a larger pattern at the Passaic County Prosecutor's Office at that time.

"You can't bisect it out," DeGroot says. "The biopsy of that (prosecutor's) office of that time is fucking malignant. It's the pieces of the mosaic. When you put them all together, it's just fucking cancerous; it really is."

Robert DeGroot

DeGroot should know. His father, John C. DeGroot, had been a detective sergeant in the town of Clifton, which borders Paterson. When he refused to go along with certain actions the prosecutor's office wanted, he suddenly found himself being charged with the contract murder of Gabriel DeFranco, whom the *New York Times* described on Oct. 26, 1968 as "a convicted gambler who was found with his throat slashed in front of his Paterson home..."

(In another coincidence, DeGroot said, his father and Rubin Carter were briefly cellmates, having been indicted by the same grand jury.)

John DeGroot and two co-defendants ultimately were acquitted in the DeFranco murder. But the case against his father made an enormous impression on Robert DeGroot, who at the time of the trial was attending Fordham University. So a few years later, when the same prosecutor's office came gunning for Hogan, it was no surprise to DeGroot.

"They (the Passaic County Prosecutor's Office) had lost my father's case," DeGroot recalls. "Now they were going after Fred. That was the mindset of that office, to try to chill participation in this (Carter/Artis) case. They were looking for any way to say Fred had done something to subvert what they felt was justice. But it just wasn't there, didn't exist. No matter how hard they tried. The fact was, they had guys (Bello and Bradley) who said different things at different times that were diametrically opposed."

Examples of the win-at-all-costs approach in that office continued well into the 1970s. Case in point: Lawrence Simmons. In 1977, Simmons was one of three men charged with the beating death of Dr. David Doktor in Paterson during a robbery as Doktor approached his car on the street.

Simmons was convicted in large part because one of the other two men charged, David Wilson, said Simmons and the third suspect beat Doktor while he, Wilson, only served as a lookout. Simmons was sentenced to life in prison, as was the third suspect. For his testimony, Wilson was granted immunity.

It wouldn't be until 1985 that Simmons would get his first appeal, owing in part to his original attorney's failure to file a motion to appeal the initial verdict and not informing Simmons of that fact.

Wilson had recanted his testimony against Simmons while serving time for an unrelated robbery in 1985, and that recantation was the basis for Simmons filing for a new trial, which the prosecutor's office vehemently opposed. Eventually, an evidentiary hearing was held, at which the judge said he did not believe Wilson's recantation, denying the motion for retrial. Appealing further, Simmons' convictions were upheld by a New Jersey appeals court.

It would not be until 1995, nearly 20 years after his original conviction, that the 3rd Circuit U.S. Court of Appeals would toss out Simmons' convictions, saying they were the result of racial bias by the prosecutor's office.

Simmons faced trial on the charges again in 1996. The jury deadlocked, and the prosecution decided to re-file the charges. In 1998, yet another trial was held. This time, Wilson recanted his recantation and went back to his original testimony. Simmons' attorney pointed out that before reversing field again, Wilson had written to prosecutors seeking their assistance in obtaining parole and also asking for money. The jury in the 1998 trial again deadlocked.

Ultimately, after additional attempts to get the verdicts reversed failed, the New Jersey Court of Appeals upheld the robbery conviction but dismissed the murder charge. In 2000, after 23 years in prison, Simmons was set free.

The parallels to the Carter-Artis case are not lost on Hogan – the testimony by a suspect the prosecution could lean on, the recantation of that testimony, and then the recantation of the recantation.

"It is so similar to what happened with Bello in the Carter-Artis case, it's almost too much of a coincidence," Hogan says.

Hogan testified at the re-trial in the Lafayette Bar and Grille case. Unfortunately, as noted before, Bello by that time had recanted his recantation. And several Carter alibi witnesses also backed away from their original statements. Add to that the New York lawyers being out of their element, and the second trial ended in convictions for Carter and Artis as well. Fortunately for them, the next step was into federal court, where their convictions were tossed.

"There was a real sense," DeGroot says, "that after New Jersey people had won Rubin and John a new trial...and Rubin wanted to go with the New York lawyers, that all these New Jersey people had put in all this effort, and everybody was just getting kicked to the curb. There was a sense of, 'Hey, how come we aren't at the dance anymore?'"

With the second trial also ending in convictions, the last gasp was going into federal court.

"And that (federal) judge that wound up with the case was the judge that cut Rubin and John loose, based on what I'd been saying for 20 years, that they were convicted based on prosecutorial misconduct and racial revenge," Hogan says.

Woven in among the court appearances related to the Lafayette murders case, there was another Carter-related legal matter that entangled Hogan. While Carter was out on bail awaiting his second trial, he attended the April 1976 heavyweight championship fight between Muhammad Ali and Jimmy Young in Baltimore. To his later chagrin, he was accompanied by Carolyn Kelley, who had become an ardent supporter of his cause and also a love interest.

Kelley claimed that Carter attacked her in their hotel room, giving press interviews from a hospital bed in Newark in which she maintained that Carter had become enraged and physically assaulted her, causing serious injuries. Among the many questions surrounding that incident was why Kelley waited until returning to Newark to seek hospitalization instead of going to the E.R. of a Baltimore hospital.

Carter was neither charged nor convicted of any crime in that matter. Later, however, in the 1990s, Kelley sued Carter, seeking a cut of his book royalties, and Hogan again was among those called to testify.

"I got involved with Freddy in early '83, through a 12-step program," says John "J.D." Doran, who represented Hogan in the Kelley civil suit. "He was very strong with others. He was the Drill Instructor, extremely good for people just coming into that 12-step program.

"Freddy asked me and I couldn't say no. It was a bullshit case. But Rubin was nervous. As strong as he was, he was glad to have people in his corner. He was insecure. Like a lot of championship fighters, I suppose."

Through it all, regardless of the various criminal and civil accusations lobbed at them, all three men – Carter, Hogan and Artis – maintained a bond forged by adversity. Each case served only to make that bond stronger.

These days, Hogan looks back, with a mixture of humor about the tribulations they faced and a regret that Carter is no longer around to lend his unique take on their longtime friendship.

"Rubin had a glass eye," Hogan says. "It was the result of a botched surgery while he was in prison. We often spoke about all the havoc that surrounded the things that Rubin, John and I did and the people it brought into our lives. And that included people accusing me of committing crimes and wanting to indict me because of that involvement.

"And I said to Rubin one time, 'I've not only been involved with the Hurricane, but I've been intricately exposed to the Hurricane, and as things have calmed down, maybe now I'll experience being in the eye of the Hurricane.' And he said, 'Well, I want you to have my eye when I die, so you can always have a piece of the Hurricane.'"

Rubin "Hurricane" Carter's glass eye on a chain, worn by Fred Hogan.

Hogan looks down as the eye hangs from a chain around his neck, and it is clear that this final gesture from his friend does, indeed, bring the calm that having this part of Rubin "Hurricane" Carter around will provide until the two meet again someday.

EIGHT

The Carter-Artis case gives birth to Centurion Ministries

(Sept. 20, 1976: 10 years and three months after the Lafayette triple murder)

The Carter-Artis case marked the first time in American history where the overturning of a murder conviction rested largely on racial discrimination in the policing and prosecutorial process. In a larger sense, however, it also raised questions about how many cases – with defendants of ALL races – could be affected by a win-at-all-costs approach by prosecutors. This led to more people, inside and outside of the legal profession, becoming interested in wrongful convictions and exonerations. One of them was a seminary student named James McCloskey, whose keen interest in the Carter-Artis case prompted him to form Centurion Ministries. His efforts, and the key role Fred Hogan played in inspiring them by paving the way for Carter and Artis' exonerations, are covered in this chapter.

"Our mission is to vindicate and free from prison those individuals in the United States and Canada who are __factually innocent__ of the

crimes for which they have been unjustly convicted and imprisoned for life or death."

Centurion Ministries Mission Statement (Emphasis ours)

The "Paoli Line" is a stretch of the Southeastern Pennsylvania Transit Authority (SEPTA) rail system that began in 1915 as the very first of the local commuter rail lines around Philadelphia to run exclusively on electric power. The only one previous to it in America was the Long Island Railroad. The trolley-like "Silverliner" train cars of the Paoli Line use a "catenary" system, in which apparatus reaches skyward like beseeching arms from the top of the car to touch live electric wires that run above the tracks, thus providing power to the train.

Traveling from the Paoli station to Center City Philadelphia takes about 45 minutes, as the train winds its way through tony suburbs like Berwyn, Devon and Villanova toward the grittier neighborhoods of the City of Brotherly Love. Just enough time to read a long front-page article from what used to be the "Today" Magazine section of the Sunday *Philadelphia Inquirer*, back when the "Inky" had aspirations of, and true potential for, challenging the *New York Times* for readers' attentions on a Sunday morning.

Such was the case for James McCloskey, on a commute from Paoli to his job managing a business in Center City Philadelphia. He'd saved the *Inquirer's* Sunday magazine to read during that commute and his attention went immediately to the cover story from September 19, 1976, entitled "Do You Know the Hurricane?" with the subtitle "Rubin Carter's Paradoxical Personality," written by Laura Murray.

By that time in the nation's Bicentennial Year, much of the country had begun to hear about Carter and the story of how he and John Artis had been charged with, and convicted of, three murders at the Lafayette Bar and Grille in Paterson, New Jersey, in 1966, convictions that rested largely on the "eyewitness testimony" of two career criminals who would later recant that testimony, and then, in the case of one of them, recant the recantation.

At that point, Carter had been freed pending a second trial, based mostly on the work of Fred Hogan, who had started looking into the case after beginning a job as an investigator with the New Jersey Office of the Public Defender in 1970. As the *Inquirer* magazine story put it: "It was (Hogan's) work that produced the evidence on which the New Jersey Supreme Court based its decision to grant Carter a new trial."

By 1976, Carter and Hogan had become great friends, and the former middleweight boxer frequently made it a point to credit Hogan as the prime force in the attention that was now being paid to his case by the likes of Bob Dylan and Muhammad Ali. (Ali, the *Inquirer* article mentioned, was in the courtroom when a judge ordered Carter freed pending a new trial.)

"I just remember reading this story and about this guy, Fred Hogan, who had put in all these countless hours, on his own time, to investigate the Carter case," McCloskey recalls. "I hadn't paid any attention to innocent people in prison, or the judicial system or criminal justice system. It was just completely out of my world. As I was reading this article, I was quite taken with the fact that, geez, (Carter) could be an innocent man, and that this guy Fred was devoting all his spare time, hundreds if not thousands of hours of investigative work, and was successful in developing new evidence that went to Rubin's innocence."

Though he didn't fully realize it at the time, the example cited in the *Inquirer* article of Hogan's persistence in the Carter case would shape McCloskey's future, as well as the futures of dozens of people convicted of murder under shaky circumstances.

"I was impressed by the fact that another human being would give of himself like that to help free somebody. It just really stuck with me that someone would be that dedicated to doing something like this. What

Fred Hogan did inspired me. I held onto the article. That just stuck with me, the Fred part of the story, and I never forgot it. At that point, I didn't think that I would, in any way, enter the world of the convicted innocent, in New Jersey or anyplace else. To me, though, it was a really impressive story of how one man sacrificed himself for another."

Fred Hogan and Jim McCloskey, founder of Centurion Ministries,
at a retirement dinner for McCloskey.

McCloskey held onto the *Inquirer* article for at least the next four years. In 1979, weary of the grind of the business world, the bachelor made a decision to enter the seminary and become a minister.

"I felt a calling to go into the ministry," he says. "At the time, I thought I was going to be a church pastor, Presbyterian. In order to do that, you go to divinity school and get a master's of divinity. That qualifies you to become ordained. So I decided to go to Princeton Theological Seminary. It had a reputation as being the best, and, at that time, it was relatively inexpensive."

As he pursued his master of divinity degree, it began to crystallize in his mind that combining the work of a ministry with the idea of trying to exonerate the wrongly convicted would be his life's calling.

But it was not as planned out as one might think. While studying at the seminary, McCloskey happened to take an assignment as a chaplain at Trenton State Prison (ironically one of the institutions in which Carter was incarcerated during his 22 years in prison) and found himself talking with a "lifer" by the name of Jorge de los Santos of Newark.

"Long story short, he convinced me that he was innocent," McCloskey says. "Then, at that point, I remembered reading about Fred and the Hurricane. And it came together. I remembered that news article and I broke it out. And I thought, 'I'll be darned. I have a situation similar to what Fred had.' Here I was, four years later, encountering an innocent person in prison, which provided me the opportunity to do what Fred did. To be honest, even if I had never heard of Fred and Carter, I would have done what I did. But it was an extra, kind of a spiritual thing to it. It fit in with my Christian beliefs as well, to serve those forsaken people."

It took McCloskey and Paul Castellero, an attorney he recruited to help, two and a half years to free de los Santos, "which was pretty quick, given my experience since then in many other cases." That involved McCloskey taking a year off from school to devote all his energies to the case and take on the role of an investigator.

His background in business, especially the extensive interviewing that went into market research in a previous assignment in Tokyo, helped in that he had already developed the interpersonal skills that are essential for investigators to get people to open up to them.

"People have to trust you, have to like you," McCloskey said. "You have to have a certain amount of affability, so that people feel, basically, comfortable and free in telling you some of their dark secrets, namely that they lied and sent an innocent man to prison years before. You go out and you interview a bunch of different people and each person has something to add or to offer, some little piece of information, or in some cases a large piece of information, and you put the puzzle together. And you develop a wealth of new evidence that goes to the truth of the matter."

De los Santos was freed in July 1983, and by that time, McCloskey's frequent visits to see him in prison had led to contact with other inmates who wanted their cases re-investigated as well.

"I had met three other lifers, Nate Walker, Rene Santana and Tomasso Vega, and I had come to believe in their innocence," he recalls. "So, now I have a little bit of a handful. Everything came together in the summer of '83. I finished my degree, got the masters of divinity, de los Santos was freed, I had met three other New Jersey lifers, and although broke, I received, like manna from heaven, a $10,000 tax-free gift from my parents, who had come into some extraordinary money, and they gave each of their three children a $10,000 gift.

"I saw this as the seed money. So rather than going on to get ordained, I decided that, you know, I think this is what God has called me to do. He's put me in this place, and opened this door, and I'm gonna go through it. And so I decided this is my life's work, not the conventional church pastor. And I established Centurion Ministries, whose sole purpose and mission was to set out to identify and try to free innocent people in prison."

From the beginning, including how "I stumbled into de los Santos and the other three heard what I was doing with him and sought me out," McCloskey has never had to go out, Diogenes-like, to seek out those who were wrongfully incarcerated. And there is a strict criteria for those whose cases Centurion Ministries will take on. It includes a vetting process that, on average, takes about five years to complete.

Authors Jeff Beach and Fred Hogan with John Artis
at the retirement ceremony for Jim McCloskey.

"We have a staff of 15 people – nine full-time and six part-time – 25 volunteers, mostly retired folk and some students. We get 1,600 letters a year from people petitioning us for help. That's not to say they're all innocent, of course. A lot of them don't really know what our criteria is, which is to, eventually, come to a belief in their total innocence."

It all starts with a letter from the inmate or someone writing on behalf of the inmate. If the latter is the case, they are told to have the inmate write a letter because Centurion wants to deal directly with that person from the very beginning. Further correspondence between a Centurion volunteer and the inmate then leads to a decision on whether a case is developing that the organization should pursue, including making sure the inmate has exhausted his or her direct appeals.

Over time, Centurion gathers the entire written record of the case

– investigative files, court transcripts, anything that could lead to an understanding of which "facts" could have led to a wrongful conviction.

"We must have that before we can even think about trying to free somebody. Trial transcripts, any hearing that has ever taken place in a courtroom, the legal briefs, the police reports, forensic reports, whatever seems relevant."

The detailed, methodical approach – "there's the tortoise and the hare, and we're the tortoise," McCloskey says – ensures the case will have been well thought-out even before Centurion makes its final commitment to seek exoneration.

The last step is a personal visit with the inmate by McCloskey and/or Kate Germond to get a feel for whether the inmate personally "is the kind of person we want to devote our resources to for a long period of time, to help free and put back on the streets. So we're interested in their character, what kind of life they led prior to their time in prison, what kind of prison record they have, what they've done with their time. By the time we come along, they're usually down for about 20 years."

To be sure, the costs involved can become very steep, even with a large cadre of volunteers helping. While a few of the 53 people (as of this writing) that Centurion has helped free to date have recouped a significant payout from the state that wrongly imprisoned them, and then donated a substantial amount to the organization, that isn't the norm.

This is not to say the freed inmates aren't grateful, and many get involved in promotional appearances and other avenues of helping to draw attention to Centurion's work. But as for financial resources, the rest of everything Centurion needs comes from individual, foundation and faith-based group donations.

"We have no independent wealth to sustain us. We're entirely dependent on the gifts from others. Now, if a person we free is successful in a civil suit, and if they choose to, we don't ask for it, but if they choose to and decide to give a certain amount of those gains to CM, then we'll accept that."

There's no such thing as an "easy" case in the world of wrongful convictions, McCloskey said, so it's hard to pick out one or two that stand out as cases where the climb was harder than usual. Yet some have more factual obstacles.

Mark Schand of Massachusetts was an example. Six eyewitnesses pegged him as the shooter in a murder case, "but as it turned out, all six were liars," McCloskey says. "They were common criminals who were in trouble with the Springfield, Massachusetts, police. We see that all the time. That's very common. Eventually, three of the six told us that they lied, and why they lied. They said the line-up was a bogus line-up, because five of the six line-up participants were drug users and street criminals and (those being asked to identify the shooter) were their criminal associates or they otherwise knew them. The only one in the line-up they didn't know was Mark Schand. Ergo, he's the guy you're going to identify."

Sometimes, a time factor will bring greater urgency to Centurion's efforts. Case in point was Clarence Bradley in Texas, in which Centurion began its field work on the case just eight days before Bradley's scheduled execution. Clearly, the first step was to secure a stay of the execution while the organization put the wheels in motion to challenge the conviction.

"Working with another investigator down there in Conrow, Texas, we brought forward the star witness against (Bradley) and he admitted that he lied, said he'd had nightmares about it and he knew that Clarence was about ready to get killed and he had stood by while the real killers took the victim away, with her screaming for help, and he ran. So he had let one innocent girl go to her death and before we knocked on his door, he was ready to let an innocent man go to his death and he was absolutely guilt-ridden about it all. I even convinced him to go on '60 Minutes' and admit that he lied. Anyway, we freed Clarence as a result of all that."

Throughout the cases Centurion has handled, one common factor that McCloskey sees is the unreliability of eyewitness identification, especially as it lends itself to police and prosecutors leading or flat-out bargaining with witnesses to say what fits their preconceived notion of the case.

As he prepared to retire in the spring of 2015 and turn the reins of Centurion over to Kate Germond, McCloskey looked back at the 30-plus years of the agency's work and sees some progress toward a more fair judicial system, but not nearly enough to eliminate wrongful convictions.

While steps like laws requiring police to videotape all interrogations and conduct double-blind photo line-ups (in which a detective not otherwise working the case shows pictures one-at-a-time to a witness) can help reduce the number of instances in which police or prosecutorial misconduct can result in miscarriages of justice, McCloskey believes that "wrongful convictions are still going to take place."

"DNA helps," he says, but notes that it has played a role in just 10 of the organization's 53 victories to date. "It can preclude, as part of the investigation, possible suspects as being the true perpetrator and save them a ton of trouble. We're working for 18 people right now, and we have one case in that 18 that has a possible DNA potential."

In preparation for his retirement, McCloskey said one thought bridges all the various cases.

"What comes to my mind is 'How the hell did we do it?' This year in particular, we've had one setback after another, which just reminds us of how difficult it is to free the innocent. And with that knowledge, based on bitter experience, I say to myself and others, 'How the hell did we ever free 53 people?' But somehow, we did. You know, hey, it's a pretty good record. Those 53 people served over 1,083 years, over a millennium, of false imprisonment before they were freed.

"I feel very good about what we have built and what we have accomplished, and especially about the process that we have set in motion to do our work."

NINE

World Wrongful Conviction Day

(Oct. 2, 2014: Approximately 48 years after the Lafayette triple murders)

One of the organizations with which Rubin Carter became intimately involved after his release from prison was the Association In Defense of the Wrongfully Convicted (AIDWYC), which has since changed its name to Innocence Canada, a Toronto-based group that works to exonerate wrongfully convicted people and to bring attention to inequities in the legal system that lead to such convictions. Carter served several years as the group's executive director before internal disagreements led him to leave. Shortly after Carter's death in April 2014, AIDWYC began preparations for its first-ever "World Wrongful Conviction Day" commemoration.

On a bright, sunny day, October 2, 2014, in Toronto, nearly 200 people from eight countries gathered at Convocation Hall at the Court of Appeals to mark the first-ever worldwide Wrongful Conviction Day, which was created and organized by the Toronto-based Association in Defense of the Wrongfully Convicted (AIDWYC).

The event featured speakers including AIDWYC leaders, several people who have been exonerated, those who have worked to overturn wrongful convictions and noted legal scholars.

And a certain former kid from the streets of Jersey City, who spoke about his involvement as the first person to investigate the Rubin Carter/John Artis case and introduced John Artis as the keynote speaker. It was a heady experience that Fred Hogan never could have imagined when he first visited his boxing hero in prison.

"It was done at a very beautiful place," Hogan says, "like something out of 'The Paper Chase,'" referencing the movie and television series that followed law students through their travails with a particularly stern professor played by John Houseman.

"Activities featured speeches, videos and other presentations on people who have been exonerated or are fighting for exoneration, how they are still struggling," Hogan said. "Some are trying to get compensated for the time they spent in prison. One guy just got out after 31 years in prison. He may not be around to file a suit, because he's got emphysema and is in bad shape.

"It was very enlightening, and they asked me if I'd make a commitment to come back next year, and I said sure. Even if I just go up there to show my support, I'd be glad to do it. It was really quite an honor to be there for me to be at the first one. It was great to see that there's such a group of, almost like an Underground Railroad. It's a long time coming if they do get united. It's no longer a mishap that it happened over here or a mistake that it happened over there. It's just pockets of this all over the world."

Hogan is aware of the many people – everyday folks and celebrities alike – that claimed central roles in the Carter/Artis case or otherwise tried to link themselves with the duo both during the time people were fighting for their release and afterward. While he harbors no resentment toward hangers-on, he clearly does not want to be around them.

"After they were set free, a lot of people became associated with them, some with good intentions and some without," he says. "I tried to divorce myself from that element of false public acknowledgment. The three of us maintained our private friendships, and that was all I ever wanted there to be."

Fred Hogan speaks at the first World Wrongful Conviction Day in 2014.

Though Rubin Carter passed away in April 2014, his death clearly would not end the ways in which his friendship with Hogan would be inexorably linked to the search for justice. Ironically, Hogan's ability to be an integral part of the event might have been more difficult if Carter were still alive.

The exoneree's relationship with AIDWYC, which he headed as Executive Director for years after his release from prison, had soured long before his death. And following a pattern in Carter's life, it was a rift that could not be mended.

"The thing with Rubin was, there was no middle ground," Hogan recalls. "You were either with him or you were against him. And if he thought you were against him, or wouldn't do something exactly his way, that was it, you were done, and there was no going back."

With Carter's death, Hogan felt the time had come to rebuild the bridge between AIDWYC and the legacy of the Carter/Artis case. So he agreed to speak at the inaugural event.

"(AIDWYC was) established before Rubin's involvement with them, but they didn't have the exposure they had once they got involved with Rubin," Hogan says. "AIDWYC really took off when Rubin became the Executive Director. He put it on the worldwide map. Rubin and John's case by far had the most notoriety around the world out of all the cases of wrongful conviction."

While news outlets in Canada were expected to highlight the event organized by their home-country's exoneration group, the breadth and depth of the media attention paid to the day surprised Hogan.

"In Canada, they already know a lot about AIDWYC," he says, "but then all these other news organizations throughout the world picked up on it, on the first Wrongful Conviction Day. AIDWYC, in Canada, gives them instant credibility because they've been around all these years.

And the other people that are partnering with them, like Centurion Ministries, become close partners with AIDWYC. It becomes more of a worldwide movement."

Hogan and Artis chat with Sabrina Butler-Porter at World Wrongful Conviction Day. Butler-Porter spent five years on Mississippi's Death Row in the death of her infant son. She was later exonerated and the death ruled the result of a kidney malady.

In retrospect, Hogan is surprised that this kind of coalescing around the principles of fairness in the judicial system has taken as long as it has.

"What went through my mind was that, I did what I did 40 years ago, and now this is just coming to a movement type of thing now," Hogan says. "I don't mean that in an egotistical way, like I was so far ahead of the curve or anything. But there has to be a beginning.

"I was 25 years old when I did what I did then, which was just me at first, for an extended period of time. People would just look at me like I was nuts. 'Yeah, right, right, they're innocent.' I look back at what's there now, at the resources that are there now, and I'm saying, 'Boy, thank god I had good instincts, and thank god I had the tenacity to do what I did, because I could've been turned off in spite of myself.'

"There was no structure. I would grab a lawyer here, we'd go to lunch there, I'd take them up to the prison. I was going around just having anybody who would talk to me about the case sit down and talk about it."

As with any issue in the criminal justice system, the complexities actually grow, not lessen, as more attention is paid to it. That, Hogan says, has made using general terms more of a challenge.

"Everybody has a different standard, because the way it can be presented in one state, it's different in one state from what it is in another state. 'Wrongfully convicted' means what? Not guilty? Not **proven** guilty? And if you're not proven guilty, does that mean you weren't given a fair trial?

"So when you get involved in different jurisdictions, you have to say, well, how do they equate that? Centurion (Ministries) has a great model, as does AIDWYC. It has to be lifers or people on Death Row who **did not do it**. Not, it was a technicality or something else. **Did not do it**! There are other organizations that do wrongfully convicted that it's, they weren't afforded their constitutional rights, there was an illegal search, whatever. Because that's all 'wrongful' under that broader meaning, too. So you have to be very descriptive and specific to what it is you're saying."

Beyond the courtroom work on specific cases, the coming together of these groups could be the start of a lobbying effort to make the system more accountable when people are wrongfully convicted.

"You've got to be very clear on what that legislation is going to look like," Hogan said. "Anything where somebody says somebody was wrongfully convicted, the first thing is, well, what is it worth to be in prison for one day? There's a knee-jerk response. Now let's look at that and say, OK, Fred Hogan was wrongfully convicted and spent 10 years in jail. Do you throw a whole bunch of money at me? What if I never made more than $20,000 in a year? Well, you deprived me of that, plus pain, suffering and that, But what is that equal to? A million dollars a month? I don't know.

"So you have to be real clear on all of that. Because otherwise, you've got people saying, 'Well I deserve a million dollars a week.' If anybody is gonna do that movement, I'd like to weigh in on that with them. There is, I sense, an opportunity to make that movement happen. I don't know exactly that anybody's looked at that, but I would like to see them do that."

Gearty, Hogan's old boss in the Monmouth County Public Defender Region, believes it's an unfortunate but necessary evil to have cases like Carter's if society can ever expect to see improvements in the judicial system.

"Some of the great reforms come from things like this," Gearty said. "There's got to be a case that draws people's attention to whatever the problem is."

John Flynn, one of the attorneys who went with Hogan to Muhammad Ali's training camp to enlist the champ's help in drawing attention to Carter's case, agreed that "the Hurricane's" story served to open the public's eyes not only to the racial divide in the courtroom, but also to the ways prosecutors can twist evidence and arguments to fit a pre-conceived notion of a particular person being guilty.

"I think it's one of the big cogs in the wheel that rolled toward an awareness among the public, where people started realizing, 'Hey, a lot of innocent people are getting convicted, and there's corruption where, just as defendants lie, prosecutors and police lie, too.'

"Prosecutors lie all the time. They do it when they say no deal was made for a cooperating witness, and as soon as they get a conviction, that guy, that cooperating witness, walks out of jail. I've tried cases where I know they've brought these guys in from jail and they've totally perjured themselves, and you prove it and juries still, maybe even more so today than back when Rubin's case was heard, they don't get it. Today, people are not inclined to believe that their law enforcement authorities are doing corrupt things."

Frank DeSevo, the longtime attorney who grew up in Jersey City a few years ahead of Hogan and who helped Hogan in some aspects of the Carter case, thinks the system itself, more so than individual prosecutors, invites abuses.

"There's always a way for the prosecutor's office to get around what they want to do, and judges are protecting that," DeSevo said. "The reality is, you make a motion to suppress certain evidence and you're going to lose those 95, 96 percent of the time. They know who the liars are. It's like, 'This guy's full of shit, but I'm gonna protect him because the system depends upon it. I'm not gonna throw out 250 bags of heroin or cocaine because the cop searched the car without a warrant.'

"The police mentality is that the ends justify the means. 'I'm getting a bum off the streets. So, I searched him without permission. So what? I probably stopped him from killing somebody.' They don't realize that when you do that, you take away the Constitution, and then the system fails. The public doesn't know. They think the judge is gonna give you a fair trial. But you're going into a trial with an uphill climb every time when you're the defense lawyer. That's why you see so many plea bargains. You gotta plead them out because you don't want to take the risk of a much stiffer sentence."

Hogan also believes that steps can and should be taken to ensure that prosecutors have both less opportunity to seek out someone to fit their theory of who committed a crime and, at the same time, to make their own cases stronger. Techniques like double-blind photo lineups and mandatory videotaping of all interrogations will both reduce chicanery in search of a quick conviction regardless of true guilt or innocence and consequently give jurors more definitive information about how certain witness statements and evidence were developed.

Hogan speaks to Tufts University students about the Carter-Artis case, as John Artis looks on.

One frequent area of contention that's unlikely to change, Hogan believes, is the use of witnesses with less-than-spotless reputations.

"When I was a cop, I always knew that you gotta take your witnesses where they come from," he says. "You're dealing with people that are breaking the law, so you're not usually gonna get a banker or some other upstanding citizen type that's gonna come forward and say, 'Yeah, that's the person who did it.' You sleep with dogs, you get fleas. You just gotta be careful that you got a flea collar on. Absolutely, though, the motive (for testifying) has to be looked at. We always would tell our clients, 'Tell us **everything** that happened to you. So when you get on the stand, you put it out there so that when you get cross-examined, it's asked-and-answered, asked-and-answered. Yes, I was guilty of **that**, but I didn't do **this**!'"

Sometimes, Hogan says, it's not the prosecution's fault that they focus on a suspect who isn't the person who committed the crime. The desire to be seen as a "tough guy" or "thug" or "gangsta" can put people in jeopardy even if they are just wannabes.

"Sometimes, people put themselves in a situation where, it's like, well I guess I was a pretty good suspect," he says. "We, for the most part, stereotype **ourselves**. You wanta go out with the prison pants, down around your ass? You wanta go out with tattoos on your neck? It's stereotyping ourselves to the point where we can put ourselves in harm's way. So, when you say, 'Well, the cops stereotyped me,' and here you've got a tattoo on your neck of the Aryan Brotherhood, or you've got the Ku Klux Klan hood or a Blank Panther (tattoo) that says, 'Kill Whitey,' I mean, **c'mon**! Now, if somebody, some witness, says, somebody went by with a tattoo fitting that description, well, it's not too far off to have the cop say, 'I'd like to talk to you.'"

TEN

John Artis receives award with Hogan by his side (almost)

(October 2, 2015: Approximately 49 years after the Lafayette triple murder)

(NOTE: There really is no more appropriate way to write this next chapter except for me to describe it as a participant. So it is written in the first person. – Jeff Beach)

My God, does that clock really say 3:40 a.m.? I have seen 3:40 a.m. many times in my adult life, but always as I was returning home from work or a night out. Waking up at this hour is not something I am accustomed to, nor particularly talented at accomplishing.

I roll to the left, then to the right, then repeat that motion several more times in order to gain enough momentum to propel myself off the floor of Fred Hogan's spare bedroom. I sleep on the floor nearly every night, at home or away, as it is the most comfortable set-up for my chronically bad lower back.

Can Fred really be in the kitchen already, in full Hogan mode, talking to himself out loud ("My shit is TIGHT! What's MY name?") I turn down an offer of coffee (not even wanting THAT much in my stomach at this hour) and hop into the shower, getting out quickly because I know how badly he wants to get on the road.

By 4:10 a.m., he is backing his red Toyota Prius out of his garage. I fold down one of the back seats, crawl into a fetal position straddling the back of that seat and the cargo area, and promptly pass out. It will be more than two hours before I regain consciousness. As I said: not my optimal time of day, at least not from the waking-up side of things.

My first glimpse of daylight is at a rest stop somewhere in north-eastern Pennsylvania. And not the good kind. Just one where there's a couple stalls in a men's room and a few vending machines. After more than two hours of traveling at an average of around 70 mph, my guess is we're somewhere close to 150 miles from Fred's home in Ocean County, New Jersey. We're about to cross into New York, on what we believed would be about an eight-hour ride to Toronto, Ontario, Canada.

So, is this a long trip once we get north of the border? Uh, no. We're driving up (well, Fred's doing all the driving) on Friday, October 2, and returning the very next morning on Saturday, October 3. What's bringing us nearly 1,300 miles round trip in less than 48 hours? It's the Second Annual World Wrongful Conviction Day in Toronto, an event conceived by the Association In Defense of the Wrongfully Convicted (AIDWYC), the group Rubin "Hurricane" Carter headed up for several years after its founders helped free him from prison.

In 2014, Fred traveled to the inaugural event alone so he could introduce John Artis to make keynote remarks. This year, in 2015, Artis would receive the new Rubin Hurricane Carter Dr. Rubin Hurricane Carter Champion of Justice Award. Since I had met John in the interim when he visited Fred in May 2015, I agreed to tag along with Fred, even though it meant what turned out to be a significant bureaucratic nightmare in getting my first-ever passport.

Fred was, well, typically Fred-like as we prepared to go to the event: staying on top of the multitude of twists and turns in my passport process (I heard it all from the Customs people: "These pictures won't do," "You need more proof of your destination," etc.); checking in with the AIDWYC folks practically daily as to the preparations; even having AAA write out a "Trip Tik" book with directions.

That last part, we should've skipped. Though it was a different route than Fred had taken to Canada before, we figured the motorist group couldn't be far off, especially considering they were putting the trip duration around the same amount of time as it normally took Fred in the past.

A little more than halfway through the trip, it became clear this route was actually going to take about three hours longer than his previous one. After almost 12 hours on the road, we arrived in Hamilton, a suburb of Toronto. Our hotel was about 45 minutes from the Law Society of Canada, where the event would be held. With little time to spare, we quickly changed and got back on the road.

But the directions we got from our hotel's front desk to the Law Society would prove as problematic as the ones from New Jersey to Canada. By the time we spent nearly an hour reversing course, and with the normally congested Friday evening traffic in downtown Toronto snarled even further by, of all things, a Taylor Swift concert, we were tied up on the road right through the end of the AIDWYC program.

Finding a parking garage took even more time. Fortunately, John and Fred stayed in touch via cell phone about the likelihood of even being able to catch up at all. At one point, when Fred assured John we were getting close, Artis' point-blank response was "I'll wait as long as it takes for you to get here."

Fred Hogan congratulates John Artis on his award from AIDWYC
(now Innocence Canada) in Toronto

Finally, around 9 p.m., Fred Hogan, and the man he helped free from prison on a bum triple-murder rap, connected in a parking area outside a hotel in downtown Toronto. It was hard to tell who was more proud as John showed Fred his award. They beamed, embraced and talked about what Carter would have thought of the honor named for him.

A little over a half-hour later, it was over, with Fred and I headed back to our hotel in Hamilton. Fred's not a late-night eater, but by that time I was starving and decided to sample some of the fare at a nearby Tim Horton's. It seems no matter where you are in upstate New York or Ontario, there's ALWAYS a nearby Tim Horton's coffee and donut shop.

Asleep around midnight, we were up and back on the road by 8 o'clock the next morning. This time, Fred took the route he was more familiar with, and we were back on New Jersey soil just a little after sundown.

As we rolled down the Garden State Parkway toward Fred's home, I found myself wondering what kind of a friendship and connection could inspire someone to drive that far, for that long on the road, to spend less than an hour celebrating a friend receiving an award, before turning right back around and heading home.

And the only answer I could think of to answer that question was... the best kind.

ELEVEN

Racial bias in New Jersey law enforcement again becomes a question

(1989: Approximately 23 years after the Lafayette triple murder)

One might think that the state where the Carter-Artis case took place would be extremely sensitive to issues of racial bias in policing. Yet, nearly a quarter century after the Lafayette Bar and Grille triple murders, the spotlight again shone on concerns about how police in the Garden State were allowing racial bias to impact traffic stops on the New Jersey Turnpike and Garden State Parkway. Much of it was tied to direction from federal law enforcement on ways to target drug trafficking. As with the Carter-Artis case and the attempts at inmate advocacy, the New Jersey Office of the Public Defender was thrust into a prominent role once again.

For much of a three-year period from 1989 through 2000, Dale Jones' life as an Assistant Public Defender for the New Jersey Office of the Public Defender (NJOPD) centered around the state's struggle to come to grips with charges of racial profiling among the ranks of its vaunted State Police force.

A public defender since 1974, and ultimately one of the agency's top central-office administrators, Jones had long heard OPD clients contend that the vehicle stops that led to their arrests were based solely on their skin color. But until the end of the 20th Century approached, the technology to access and assess thousands of stops and arrests each year simply did not exist. And without such hard data, contentions of stops based on race came down to the word of the arresting officer versus that of the defendant.

"We knew there were many more of these, what we call 'pretext stops,' among minority motorists," Jones says. "The officer will make a stop based on something like, 'Oh, there was something dangling from the mirror,' or, "It didn't look like they had their seat belt on.' When you go into court and try to suppress evidence from that kind of stop, the judge will always take the word of the police officers."

The first cases to begin attracting attention were filed by the Middlesex County division of the NJOPD. Middlesex is a sprawling, largely urban and suburban county anchored by New Brunswick, the home of Rutgers University. The two major thoroughfares that would become central to the profiling case, the New Jersey Turnpike and Garden State Parkway, run through the county. The early Middlesex County cases alleged, as those following them also would, that motorists were being stopped solely because of their race.

A state Superior Court judge would rule that each of the more than 200 cases in which racial profiling was claimed by defendants needed to be reviewed on a case-by-case basis. With computer databases capable of accessing reams of police and court records in a way that an individual attorney working with paper records never could hope to, the tools were finally there, Jones said, to analyze, through hard statistics, how minority drivers were being stopped at a far greater rate than their population would suggest was plausible by sheer chance.

"That type of work could only come about because of the type of work the Public Defender's Office in New Jersey was able to do, because it is a statewide office," says Jones, who retired from the organization in March 2015. "Because it's a statewide office, you have the ability through computerized records and databases to assess all the records you would need to in order to make that case. No single attorney could mount that kind of a challenge."

Dale Jones (Photo credit: Ashley Garrett)

Throughout the 1990s, the cases would exist in relative obscurity, of interest mainly to the lawyers, law enforcement officials and defendants involved. But the issue came to more widespread public attention in 1998, when two state troopers stopped four young minority men in a van on the Turnpike and opened fire on the van when, they said, it began to back up toward them in a threatening way. That sparked a lawsuit by the four van occupants that brought "racial profiling" into the lexicon of average New Jersey residents for the first time.

By 1999, as media and federal government scrutiny of State Police stops mounted, the state's Attorney General was releasing statistics showing that 75 percent of drivers arrested on the New Jersey Turnpike were minorities, and then-Attorney General (later State Supreme Court Justice) Peter Verniero stated that racial profiling was "real – not imagined."

Shortly thereafter, the federal Department of Justice installed a monitor whose job it was to oversee a State Police effort to reverse the practice of racial profiling, an arrangement that would last until 2009.

But the federal government itself was not without blame in creating the environment that spawned racial profiling in New Jersey and elsewhere, as Jones and others pointed out at the time. Racial profiling was largely a child of the federal "War on Drugs," and specifically the Drug Enforcement Administration's "Operation Pipeline," which established racially based "profiles" of drug couriers, with blacks and Hispanics overwhelmingly represented among those being targets (with the exception of acknowledging white-dominated motorcycle gangs' role in distributing methamphetamine). Add to that what was already a longstanding reputation of two major highways, the New Jersey Turnpike and Garden State Parkway (both patrolled by the State Police) as major routes for drugs from Florida to New York City, and the recipe was set for racial profiling in the state.

"The fact of the matter is," Jones says, "two-thirds of the 80,000 or so cases a year in the Public Defender's office are possession or distribution of narcotics, and the vast majority of them are disposed of by plea agreement. When you see this kind of burden placed on the court system, you have to question the wisdom of the 'War on Drugs,' this burden of arresting, prosecuting and warehousing of drug offenders in state prisons."

Through the 1980s and 1990s, Jones says, the pursuit of being seen as an "effective" state trooper was largely tied to how many drug arrests, often through pretext stops, a trooper was making. That, Jones says, led to a culture where racial profiling was seen as an asset, not a detriment. Jones acknowledges now that the NJOPD had a "mole" in the State Police who was helping the attorneys establish that the numbers they were compiling also had a corresponding impact on how many of the state troopers approached their jobs. Largely overlooked as part of the racial profiling issue was a lawsuit filed by a group of black state troopers in 1993 alleging that they were subject to racially motivated hazing by white troopers, denied job transfers and promotions and, for those who spoke up about the situation, sent to assignments far from their homes.

"Yes, I will tell you that we did have a 'mole' in the State Police," Jones says. "There were troopers who did not like what was going on and were willing to talk to us. And what they told us was that there was a culture where those who were playing it straight were not getting promoted, they were being ostracized by other troopers. But fortunately, there **were** people in the State Police willing to give us that information."

That, combined with the hard data on traffic stops, helped the NJOPD make its case to the federal government. However, they were only part of the reason New Jersey's public defenders were able to establish the existence of racial profiling, Jones says. First, there had to be the concept that the criminal justice system had an inherent bias against minority defendants. That, Jones contends, took a giant leap forward in the Rubin Carter/John Artis case.

"I think that (Carter/Artis) case has cultural significance for two reasons," Jones says. "First, that case really brought to the forefront all those factors of how much race and racism plays a role in the criminal justice system," Jones says. "I don't know that we ever would have gotten to the point of a concept like racial profiling if we hadn't had cases like Rubin Carter's that showed the bias in the system. The significance of that case is that it was clearly a product of a racist approach to policing. Secondly, it is emblematic of what is still going on in the United States today, with unarmed black men being shot by police.

Hogan, Carter and Dale Jones

"A statewide Public Defender system brings you the resources that can help level the playing field when you're facing off in court with the government, which has all the resources. But those resources have to be coupled with people like Fred (Hogan) who are willing to go the extra mile."

While Jones is proud of the work he and others accomplished in the New Jersey racial profiling issue, he holds no illusions about the role of race being eliminated in the modern criminal justice system.

"I came in to the Public Defender's Office in 1974," he says, "and all you had to do then was sit in any criminal court in Essex County (the New Jersey county that include the state's largest urban center, Newark) and see who and why they prosecuted. Discretion played, and still does play, a role in the charging process. And even though we took great strides with the racial profiling cases in New Jersey, that still dealt only with the State Police. It never touched on the hundreds of local police departments and their practices."

An underlying factor that Jones sees as potentially never changing in the way criminal law is adjudicated is the simple fact that judges, with very few exceptions, will assume the veracity of a police officer's testimony over that of the person charged in the case.

"I think there is a realization," Jones said, "by everybody involved in the criminal justice system, even defense attorneys, that if judges begin to say police officers lack credibility, the criminal justice system will begin to fall apart. Even in the narcotics cases, many of the searches do result in the finding of contraband. The police do show up in court with the contraband. And unless it was planted, there *was* contraband. So even if you can show the search that resulted in the contraband wasn't constitutionally justified, people will still say, 'Well, he got off on a technicality.' There is no fundamental faith in the Fourth Amendment."

TWELVE

Bringing "The Hurricane" full circle by delivering on a promise

(June 2015: Almost 50 years after the Lafayette Bar and Grille murders)

When Rubin "Hurricane" Carter passed away in 2014 from cancer, his co-defendant John Artis and the investigator who first delved into their case hoping to prove wrongful convictions, Fred Hogan, knew they were bound to continue the work the three had done to help exonerate others over three decades since Carter's release. It was not only a philosophical commitment to the core tenets of judicial fairness, but also a deeply personal obligation to the man whose fight for justice is a historical landmark in America. Part of that personal commitment entailed taking Carter's cremated ashes on a trip the boxer always wanted to take, but never got the chance.

The distance from Paterson, N.J. to Clarksdale, Miss., is 1,166 miles, basically a two- or three-day trip by car.

While Paterson epitomizes the former industrial powerhouses of the Northeast that have fallen on hard times as industries and commerce moved out to the suburbs and other regions of the country, Clarksdale, as might be expected, has a more rural feel to it, even though its 17,000 residents share, or have previously shared mutual employers.

Paterson, meanwhile, was founded as the epicenter of America's industrial revolution by a society headed by Alexander Hamilton, and became known as "The Silk City" for its key role in creating that fabric for U.S. customers.

But Paterson – the New Jersey municipality that ranks second only behind New York City in population density per square mile for towns over 100,000 – and the quintessential Mississippi Delta town of Clarksdale, both factored prominently in the life of Rubin "Hurricane" Carter. Paterson, for the obvious reason of it being the site of the Lafayette Bar and Grille triple murder case that centered on Carter and John Artis, and Clarksdale, as the site of a story that fascinated Carter, the legendary "Crossroads," the intersection of Highways 61 and 49, where Delta Blues pioneer Robert Johnson was said to have sold his soul to the devil for success in the music industry (a plan which, if true, went awry, as Johnson died at age 27 in 1938 without much critical acclaim, long before his recordings would resurface and gain attention as rock stars like Eric Clapton began to speak of his influence on their guitar playing in the '60s and '70s).

As a jazz and blues aficionado, Carter had often spoken with Artis and Hogan about his desire to one day make a pilgrimage to the Crossroads. They also were aware that actor and activist Morgan Freeman was part-owner of a nearby jazz and blues club called "Ground Zero," (founded in May 2001, several months before the term "ground zero" would take on a whole different meaning throughout America).

"Rubin and John knew about it because of their connection to the music, and we all used to talk about making this trip down to the Delta," Hogan said. "It's funny, because I had also had such conversations with (then-New Jersey Public Defender Stanley) Van Ness about going to the Delta.

"But there was never an opportunity. Life gets in the way, as they say. When I went up to see Rubin near the end (of his life) and John and I started getting Rubin's affairs in order, it became something we felt we had to put on the front burner once we got past all the immediate stuff we were dealing with.

"I'd talked about doing it with Van Ness, then he died. I'd talked about doing it with Rubin, then he died. So, John and I started thinking, 'Well, we better do this before we both die, too.'"

Fred Hogan and John Artis traveling to the Mississippi Delta

(Author's note: While their trip was in the planning process, Jeff Beach learned while at a meeting in Biloxi, Miss., that a short drive away from Clarksdale was a rural outpost known as Merigold, and just outside Merigold was the last known true "juke joint" in the Delta, known as "Po Monkey's," a former sharecropper house where true Delta blues music was kept alive by a series of private parties almost nightly and a Thursdays-only open, public night where anyone could visit. So, Hogan and Artis added Po' Monkey's to their itinerary.)

"It's basically in the middle of the middle of the middle of nowhere," Hogan said. "You can't get any more down the end of a dirt road than this place. All the times I'd talked with anybody about going to the Delta, I'd always visualized a shack at the end of dirt road to get the flavor of the Delta. Then Po Monkey's popped up. And it was what I had visualized for 35 years."

While on the tour, Artis couldn't resist indulging in his love for the drums, which he got the chance to display during the visit to Ground Zero.

"Only at Ground Zero did we make it known about John being Rubin's co-defendant, since we didn't want it to be all about that, the case and all that," Hogan said. "A couple people asked if he was Morgan Freeman (they bear a passing resemblance). One waitress came over and we talked a bit about who John was, then she brought some other people over and they introduced themselves, making something of a fuss over him.

"But then John would turn and point at me and say, 'This is the guy that started it all.' So, after we got talking to the people there a bit, that's when John got up and started playing the drums."

Beyond the music and the sightseeing, Artis and Hogan had a more meaningful mission. Hogan wore Carter's prosthetic eye (the one he has mounted on a chain) so that, in a way, Carter could "see" the places they had talked about visiting together but never got the opportunity to do so. And Artis brought some of Carter's cremated ashes to spread at sites he knew his friend had wanted to visit, but had never gotten the chance.

"We decided that when we made the trip, I'd bring the eye with me and that would mean part of Rubin was there," Hogan said. "John said, I'll bring some ashes. So, everywhere we went, we spread some ashes. In, Georgia, Alabama, Mississippi, at Po Monkey's, Ground Zero, and at The Crossroads."

*Fred Hogan visits the famed "Crossroads"
to spread some of Rubin Carter's ashes.*

Hogan doesn't see the trip as an "end" or a "final chapter" in the six-decade connection among the three men and their search to see a justice system that truly is just.

"It was simply a continuum," he said, "of fulfilling a promise we made to our friend. It's just something that friends do, you follow through on what you talked about and what you said you were going to do."

Acknowledgments

Copy Editing/Proofreading – Jacqueline Turner, Dale Jones, Art Penn, Gerald Boswell

Tufts University's Dr. Rubin "Hurricane" Carter Archives – Erin Kelly, Daniel Santamaria, Pat Williams, Pamela Hopkins

Additional support and guidance: Colin Asher, Selwyn Raab, Jim Hirsch, Dave Anderson, Win Wahrer, Wanda Moore, Dr. DuWayne Battle, Michael Murphy, James N. Butler Jr. and Ray Ortiz

The owners, employees and patrons of Ground Zero blues club (Clarksdale, Miss.) and Po' Monkey's (Merigold, Miss.)

About the Authors

Fred W. Hogan, a former policeman who switched careers early to become an investigator for the New Jersey Office of the Public Defender (NJOPD), put his investigative skills to work paving the way for the exoneration of wrongfully convicted boxer Rubin "Hurricane" Carter and his co-defendant John Artis in the 1966 triple murder at the Lafayette Bar and Grille in Paterson, N.J. The U.S. Army veteran retired after 40 years with the NJOPD, having filled roles as both an investigator and Statewide Drug Court Coordinator. He now lives in Lakewood, N.J. and serves as the President of the Council on Compulsive Gambling of New Jersey and is a past president of the substance-abuse counseling group New Jersey Lawyers Concerned for Lawyers. He has two sons and seven grandchildren, and devotes much of his time to addiction-counseling efforts and promoting military veterans' issues.

Jeff Beach spent 15 years in print journalism, where he was honored with seven statewide and regional journalism awards, before becoming the public information officer for the NJOPD in 1999, where he met and became colleagues and friends with Fred Hogan. Since 2004, he has been a public information officer, policy advisor and emergency management coordinator for the New Jersey Department of Agriculture. He served in 2012 as the national President for the Communications Officers of State Departments of Agriculture (COSDA). He is the father of two daughters and is active in efforts to reverse public bias against pit bulls.